English Ceramics 1580–1830

English Ceramics 1580–1830

A Commemorative Catalogue
of ceramics and enamels
to celebrate the 50th Anniversary
of the English Ceramic Circle
1927-1977

R. J. Charleston and Donald Towner

Sotheby Parke Bernet Publications
London 1977

Committee Members

ERRATA

Please note that the following captions have
become transposed:
234 with 235 and
221 with 225

© R. J. Charleston and Donald Towner 1977

Published by
Philip Wilson Publishers Limited
for
Sotheby Parke Bernet Publications
Russell Chambers, Covent Garden, London WC2

Edited by Paul J. Mack, Sotheby Parke Bernet & Co.
Design by Graphikos Design Consultants Limited, London
Phototypesetting by Galleon Photosetting, Ipswich
Reproduction by Typerian Limited, Ipswich
Printed and bound in Great Britain by
Butler and Tanner Limited, Frome

Contents

List of Lenders

Mr and Mrs T. D. Barclay
Mr and Mrs Franklin A. Barrett
Mrs Doreen Bayley
Edward Behar Esq
Norman E. Bell Esq
Mr and Mrs P. G. Bennett
Eric Benton Esq
Miss Mavis Bimson
I. M. Booth Esq
C. Bosanquet Esq
Anthony du Boulay Esq
H. Gilbert Bradley Esq
Dr Peter Bradshaw
Mrs K. Brown
T. G. Burn Esq
Mr and Mrs Francis Burrell
G. T. Bushell Esq
Alan Caiger-Smith Esq
Dr J. A. Campbell
J. G. Cattley Esq
R. J. Charleston Esq
Mr and Mrs T. P. P. Clifford
David Coke-Steel Esq
L. A. Compton Esq
R. S. Copeland Esq
Mrs Robin Craven
Peter Davis Esq
Mrs Una des Fontaines
D. Drakard Esq
Geoffrey A. L. Freeman Esq
W. J. Grant-Davidson Esq
G. E. A. Grey Esq
Stephen Hanscombe Esq
Mrs Z. Hodgson
Mr and Mrs David Holgate
Mr and Mrs John Howell
Sir Leslie Joseph
Dr R. Kemp
A. J. B. Kiddell Esq
Dr J. B. Kurtz
L. L. Lipski Esq
Mr and Mrs J. V. G. Mallet
Mrs M. M. Newton
P. Pryce Esq
Mr and Mrs M. I. Pulver
Lady Reigate
Mr and Mrs Denis Blake Roberts
P. Scarisbrick Esq
Mrs F. Shand-Kydd

C. D. Sheaf Esq
Ronald Sillito Esq
Mr and Mrs R. S. Sparrow
E. N. Stretton Esq
Mrs D. and I. Sutherland
Mr and Mrs H. Talbot
Mrs J. B. Tatchell
The Rev. D. J. D. Thornton
A. Thwaite Esq
H. G. Timms Esq
D. C. Towner Esq
Mrs Nancy Valpy
O. Van Oss Esq
T. G. Walford Esq
Dr Bernard M. Watney
F. T. Wheeldon Esq
S. Williams Esq
D. E. Zeitlin Esq

Preface

When the English Porcelain Circle (from 1931 the English Ceramic Circle) was founded in 1927 there were forty-five members, none from overseas. Now, fifty years later, we have close on five hundred members of whom over a hundred are from the United States of America. A flourishing Society indeed, with a remarkable record for research and publication; its authorative *Transactions* having remained at a high level of ceramic scholarship. Our Society spends all its income on the annual publication of the *Transactions* and, with no reserve funds, is having to increase the subscription to maintain its traditional standard of excellence.

Originally the Circle met in its members' homes and, more recently, in the lecture theatres of the Victoria and Albert and other Museums, to all of whom we are greatly indebted. With the closing of the Museum at the Wellcome Foundation, which offered us hospitality for several years, our unique library is now in store for an indefinite period and inevitably bequests are yearly becoming fewer. We urgently need somewhere in London where we can set out our library treasures once again.

This present Golden Jubilee Exhibition would not have been possible had it not been for the generosity of Sotheby Parke Bernet & Company, who have spared no effort in surmounting the many difficulties that arose at every stage. This is particularly the case because our plans to hold the exhibition at the Victoria and Albert Museum were well advanced when it was announced by the Director that, owing to Government cut-backs, they would have to be abandoned. A munificent grant of £1,400 by the Board of Trustees of the Swiss *Ceramica – Stiftung* has enabled us to illustrate this important Catalogue with sixteen fine colour plates. We will remain forever grateful for this wonderful altruism.

When the Society came of age in 1948 the first Exhibition was held in the Victoria and Albert Museum. This aroused sufficient interest to increase the membership from one hundred and twenty-six to one hundred and fifty-seven in the same year. The main Catalogue was not published until after the Exhibition; however, in spite of rather brief descriptive entries, it has remained an important source of reference. The fine half-tone plates illustrate every piece with great clarity although the number of exhibits was twice that in the present Exhibition. Then, as now, the objects on show were all from member's private collections, chosen initially by members themselves. It is instructive to compare the relative numbers of exhibits from particular factories in the two exhibitions. On the porcelain side, for example, Worcester still predominates, but we now have relatively much more space devoted to the Liverpool factories, and Caughley is considered respectable enough to be included.

Although some of the important large collections which were represented in the twenty-first Anniversary Catalogue have now been wholly or partially dispersed, it is noteworthy how many are extremely well represented in major museums throughout the country: the H. R. Marshall Worcester Collection, for example, at Oxford, the Lord and Lady Fisher Collection at Cambridge and the Dyson Perrins Collection at Worcester. We still have our important, large collections, some of which are represented in this Exhibition; however, the average member of the Circle acquires pieces on a more modest scale. People are now more knowledgeable than they were twenty-nine years ago; there is more competition and much less chance of finding rarities at a bargain price. Less money is available in the United Kingdom, but saleroom prices of fine quality pieces continue to climb.

Collectors by their very nature are individualists and members of the English Ceramic Circle, being no exception, have tended also, in the past, to carry out research on the same basis and to be somewhat jealous of their particular field. More and more, however, team-work is becoming necessary for research, especially in the realm of industrial archaeology. In recent years there have been a number of papers in the Circle's *Transactions* written by two or more members and gaining in importance thereby.

This Catalogue is likely to have far reaching effects as a guide for the collector of the future and to remain an invaluable source of reference for the amateur and professional alike. It has been compiled by two foremost authorities on ceramics, Robert Charleston and Donald Towner, and it gives a fascinating insight into the contemporary taste for English Porcelain, Enamels and Earthenware. Every piece on exhibition is illustrated, described in detail and set in its appropriate historical background. References to the literature abound and, being brought together in this way, give a new insight into the important research undertaken by members of the English Ceramic Circle over the past fifty years.

This Golden Jubilee Catalogue proves that members have not been content merely to amass collections. They have set themselves to carry out fundamental investigations into every aspect of the subject, whether it is historical and stylistic assessment, or the study of ceramic techniques, industrial archaeology or archival research.

Our cordial thanks are due to all those members of the Circle who have lent pieces and have subscribed towards the cost of this anniversary venture. The Exhibition Committee have carried out their part with great determination, working in full co-operation with members of Sotheby's staff who, in turn, have collected the exhibits together, photographed them and helped us display them at their Belgravia Rooms.

Bernard Martyn Watney
President of the English Ceramic Circle

PLATE I

1 A silver-mounted Malling Jug

PLATE II

8 A tin-glaze Posset-pot and Cover

PLATE III

38   A Staffordshire salt-glaze Figure of Mezzetin

PLATE IV

PLATE V

66 **A pair of Ralph Wood Figures of a Stag and a Hind**

PLATE VI

**79 A Yorkshire creamware
Commemorative Jug**

PLATE VII

**94, 95 Two creamware Screw-top Boxes and a
Cup and Saucer**

PLATE VIII

118 A Chelsea Teapot and Cover

PLATE IX

128 Three Chelsea Figures of 'Ranelagh Masqueraders'

PLATE X

**133 A Bow Tureen and Cover in the
form of a Duck**

PLATE XI

真前雨
黍前黍

**136   A Bow Group of the Goddess
Ki Mao Sao and Worshippers**

PLATE XII

144 A Derby Perfume-burner in the
form of a Dovecote

PLATE XIII

169   A Worcester 'Cabbage-leaf' Jug

PLATE XIV

182 A Liverpool (William Ball)
Vase and Cover

PLATE XV

**202 A New Hall part Tea Service painted by
Fidelle Duvivier**

PLATE XVI

244–246 Three London Enamel Patch Boxes

Introduction

Pottery Section

The catalogue entries and arrangement of exhibits in the Pottery section inevitably follow a different pattern from those in the Porcelain section. The latter is most readily divided into factories whereas the pottery could be divided either by period, or by material – and this seems to be the most logical and simple way. Four main categories have therefore resulted according to whether the ware is stoneware or earthenware and then as to how it has been glazed, whether tin-glazed earthenware, salt-glazed stoneware, lead-glazed earthenware or unglazed stoneware. It has been possible to subdivide some of these. Of course where factories or potters are known or suspected, these are stated but do not affect the main divisions. This system introduces a few anomalies, such as classing very early wares with late in some instances, but even so there is the link of the same material.

In accepting offers of the loan of pieces of pottery for the exhibition, the whole field of English earthenware and stonewares was kept in view so that the exhibits catalogued here not only show some of the finest specimens from members' collections, but also exhibit the development and change of styles which extend from about 1580 to 1830, a period of two hundred and fifty years. The choice of these pieces has rested with the Exhibition Selection Committee, whose main endeavour has been to cover as large a part of the whole field of English pottery before 1830 as possible rather than select the rarest pieces, though these naturally carried weight. To be able to present an almost complete picture of English pottery within the space of a little more than a hundred exhibits is most remarkable and shows the great variety of interests possessed by members of The English Ceramic Circle.

The Exhibition suitably starts with the magnificent Malling Jug with its lovely form and colouring with silver mounts, which can be dated between 1580 and 1590. The arms depicted on the cover are those of the Cochrane family. The other pieces of tin-glazed earthenware cover a wide variety of fine pieces which include tiles, a monteith, a posset-pot, some handsome bowls and vases, as well as finely painted plates and dishes.

The next section, Salt-glazed Stoneware, is rich in the early drab-coloured ware with brown staining. There are two notable examples from Dwight's pottery at Fulham, pieces from Staffordshire and a fine Nottingham mug. In white salt-glaze there is a great variety, including some very notable pieces. Mention must be made of the very fine pew-group, arbour-group and other figures. Of outstanding interest is the Littler teapot with white enamelling on the blue glaze also a beautiful pair of swans and a white owl. Scratch-blue and a great variety of enamelled pieces are also included.

Lead-glazed earthenware is well represented in all its many sub-divisions from slipware to nineteenth century blue-printed wares. These include country-made wares of varying dates, some very fine examples of the so-called Astbury type of ware, colour-glazed wares of the Wedgwood-Whieldon partnership and some outstanding examples of the work of Ralph Wood, especially fine are a pair of seated deer. Under the subheading of Creamware practically the whole field of this class of ware is covered, from the early deep cream-coloured wares both plain and enamelled to the later paler creamwares, pearlwares and white wares.

The last section comprises the unglazed stonewares ranging from those of the Elers brothers, who are well represented by a fine teapot and mug, to the mid-eighteenth century redware and black basalt ware followed by examples of Wedgwood and Turner jasperware and white unglazed stoneware. Truly a good heritage.

D.C.T.

Tin-glazed Earthenware

1 Jug
London, probably Aldgate, second half of
16th century, Malling type
Height 10½ in (26.7 cm)

The tin-glazed body is powdered with brown
and blue. It has a fitted silver cover of
1580–1590, surmounted by a squirrel which
forms the knob. The silver cover is incised with
a coat-of-arms and birds and flowers. There is
also a fitted silver chased rim round the base.
The arms are those of a branch of the family of
Cochrane.

See colour plate I

2 Monteith
English, second half of 17th century
Diameter 12 in (30.5 cm); height 6¾ in (17 cm)

Fixed ring handles from lions' heads. Eight
openings in the rim.
Chinese figures and landscapes painted in blue,
yellow and orange.

Previously in the Gautier Collection.

3 Vase
English, second half of 17th century
Height 14¼ in (36.3 cm)

Ogee shape.
Painted in blue with Chinese flowers and birds.

4 Urn
English, second half of 17th century
Height 13⅛ in (33.5 cm); diameter at top
12½ in (32 cm)

Two strap handles and pie-crust edge, painted
in blue with Chinese motifs.

5 Charger
Probably Lambeth, last quarter of 17th century
Diameter 13½ in (34.5 cm)

Tin-glazed earthenware with lead-glazed back.
Painted with a 'tulip' design in green, blue,
yellow and orange with a 'blue dash' border.

6 Plate
Perhaps Lambeth or Liverpool, about 1689
Diameter 8½ in (21.5 cm)

Painted in blue, ochre and brown with a double
portrait of William and Mary, inscribed 'WMR'.

From the Sidebotham and Garner Collections.

7 Plate
Perhaps Lambeth or Liverpool, about 1702
Diameter 8½ in (21.5 cm)

Painted in blue and black with a portrait of
Queen Anne within a formal border.

8 Posset-pot
Bristol or London, first quarter of 18th century
Height 9⅛ in (23.3 cm)

Two strap handles and spout, mushroom knob
to cover.
Floral painting in blue, red and green.

See colour plate II

9 Teapot
Probably Lambeth, about 1740
Height 3½ in (9 cm)

Globular with wish-bone handle, short spout
and ball knob.
Painted in blue with scroll motifs and a band **of**
diaper pattern round the top.

10 Punch-bowl
Perhaps Bristol, about 1740
Height 4½ in (11 cm); diameter 10¾ in
(27.5 cm)

Painted in blue with a drinking scene after
Hogarth inscribed 'A Midnight Modern
Conversation', surrounded by a fruiting vine
and a border of small scenes with a diaper
pattern between. On the outside, a continuous
landscape. The rim is coloured red.

11 Punch-bowl
Bristol, about 1740
Diameter 9 in (23 cm); height 4 in (10.2 cm)

Decorated in blue with birds and flowers on the
outside. The interior has a two-masted ship in
full sail, the flags are touched with red. There is
a floral border. Below the ship is the inscription
'Success to the new Friend Ship'.

12 Punch-bowl
English Delft, perhaps Bristol or Wincanton,
about 1740
Height 5⅝ in (14.5 cm); diameter 12 in
(30.5 cm)

The outside has a powdered manganese ground
with shaped reserves in which are blue painted
flowers and insects. The interior is blue-painted
with a mimosa and fence design.

13 Frame of Four Tiles
Liverpool, printed by John Sadler, about 1756
Each tile is 5 in square

Printed in blue from wood-blocks.
Tiles 1, 2, and 3 are rococo designs from a
series of prints entitled '*Caffe, The und Tobac
Zierathen*' by J. E. Nilson of Augsburg.
Tile 4 is a Chinoiserie subject taken from a
print illustrated in *ECC Trans*, vol 9, pt 1,
1973, Anthony Ray, *Liverpool Printed Tiles*,
pl 31A.

Illustrated in *Antique Collector*, February 1970,
p IX.

14 Vase
Bristol, about 1750
Height 6½ in (16.5 cm)

Lion's head masks as handles.
Painted in blue with a house in a Chinese
landscape.

A similar vase is illustrated in Garner and
Archer, *English Delftware*, London, 1972, pl 97.

15 Plate
Bristol, 1760–1770
Diameter 12 in (30.5 cm)

Scalloped edge with *bianco sopra bianco* border
painted with a Chinese landscape with a high
rock in blue.

16 Tile
Liverpool, about 1760
5 in (12.7 cm) square

Painted in polychrome colours of blue, green,
yellow, red-brown and purple with flowers in a
blue and white bowl.

Illustrated in Ray, *English Delftware Tiles*,
col pl D and 523 on p 221.

Formerly in the Hodgkin Collection.

17 Puzzle-jug
Lambeth, 1766
Height 9¼ in (23.5 cm)

The cylindrical neck is pierced with interlacing circles. The rim has three nozzles and the underside of the hollow looped handle is pierced. It is painted in blue with flowering peonies below a formal trellis and cracked ice border. The handle is also inscribed underneath with the date 1766.

Formerly in the Berry and Garner Collections.

18 Urn
English, middle 18th century
Diameter at top 8⅞ in (22.2 cm); height 10 in
(25.5 cm)

Two scrolled handles, painted in blue with
European figures in a landscape.

19 Plate
Bristol, about 1760
Diameter 8¾ in (22 cm)

Scalloped rim, painted with a landscape in blue with buildings and men fishing. It has a *bianco sopra bianco* border.

An identical plate is illustrated in Garner and Archer, *English Delftware*, London, 1972.

Previously in the Arthur Lane Collection.

20 Dish
Lambeth, about 1760
Diameter 8½ in (21.5 cm)

Painted in the centre with a Chinese landscape
in blue and manganese. A wide border has a
scratched white decoration on a powder-blue
ground.

Illustrated in Garner, *English Delftware*, pl 67B
and in ECC 1948 Exhibition *Catalogue*, pl 7,
no 29.

Formerly in the Hemming, Ragg, and Garner
Collections.

Salt-glazed Stoneware

21 Mug

John Dwight, Fulham Pottery, about 1685
Height 4 in (10 cm)

Globular body, horizontally reeded neck and
grooved loop handle with small scroll below.
Metal-mounted rim marked with 'H' in script.
Greyish-white body with slight speckling.

Illustrated in Geoffrey Wills, *English Pottery and
Porcelain*, 1969, p 68, fig 3.

Two mugs of this type are in the Schreiber
Collection each having a silver collar engraved
with the initials SS and date 1682.

22 Tavern Bottle

John Dwight, Fulham Pottery, late 17th century
Height 8 in (20.3 cm)

Simple loop handle, stringing round top of neck
stained brown. On the front a round applied
medallion bearing a cock facing to the left,
surrounded by the inscription 'W. Morrison.
Temple-Bar'.

A similar bottle in the London Museum is
illustrated in *ECC Trans*, vol 5, pt 2, 1961,
pl 119.

23 Tankard
Probably London, 1737
Height 8½ in (22 cm)

The top half stained brown, the lower half drab.
Wide loop handle turned over at the base. A
silver band round the rim. Moulded decoration
of a stag-hunt with sportsmen and dogs, two
ale-houses and rosettes. In the centre is a scene
of four men seated at a table smoking and
drinking punch. Above is incised the
coat-of-arms of the Armourer's Company with
the inscription 'Tho sparrow att
Chippenham 1737'.

24 Two Handled Tankard
Possibly a Staffordshire pot-house, about 1740
Height 7½ in (19 cm)

Drab in colour with very little brown staining
showing. Applied moulded decorations of a
hunt with dogs, followers on horse-back, a
huntsman, birds, trees, an ale house and the
'sun in splendour'.

25 Bowl
Perhaps Staffordshire, 18th century
Height 3 in (17.5 cm); diameter 13½ in
(34.2 cm)

The shallow bowl contains a rouletted design of
a cock against a background of foliage. Stained
brown.

Formerly in the Allman Collection.

26 Mug

James Morley, Nottingham, about 1700
Height 4¾ in (12 cm)

Globular with double walls, the outer wall being
pierced with sprays of flowers with the stems
incised. Horizontally reeded neck, loop handle.
Covered with a rich brown slip.

Referred to in *ECC Trans*, vol 9, pt 2, 1974 by
Adrian Oswald, 'Nottingham and Derbyshire
Stoneware', p 189.

Exhibited at the Exhibition of British
Salt-glazed Stoneware, Morley College,
November 1972.

These carved jugs are illustrated in an
advertisement issued by James Morley at 'Ye
Pot-House in Nottingham.'

27 Two Mugs

Probably Staffordshire, about 1740
Height 4¾ in (11.5 cm) and 2½ in (16.5 cm)

These two mugs are identical in form and
colour, which is a pale-grey, but are of
considerably different sizes. Strap handle with
pinched end.

28 Pew-group
Staffordshire, about 1740
Height 7¾ in (19.6 cm); width 7 in (17.8 cm)

White with brown markings. A central seated lady has a pug-dog on her lap. She wears a frilled cap and striped skirt. She has brown eyes, cheeks and collar and is flanked by two bewigged gentlemen with white frogged brown waistcoats with white buttons. One holds a brown snuff-box and the other rests his right hand on the lady's shoulder. They have brown shoes with white buckles. The Victoria and Albert Museum specimen lacks the pug-dog, while the British Museum specimen, also without a dog, has the arms of the gentlemen differently arranged.

29 Mustard-pot

Probably Staffordshire, about 1743
Height 3 in (7.5 cm)

Formed as a bear holding its young one. The
head is removable and when placed upside-
down forms a receptacle for mixing the
mustard. It has a loop handle on one side.
Decorated with dark-brown manganese spots.
Salt-glaze jugs as bears with removable heads to
form cups are well-known, but the present
mustard pot is probably the smallest example of
a salt-glaze bear yet found.

30 Teapot

Thomas and John Wedgwood, Big House,
Burslem, about 1745
Height 6 in (15.3 cm)

Slip-cast, diamond shaped with contracted
moulded foot. Notched loop handle, spout with
reliefs of two cherubs' heads and serpents
terminating in an animal's head with open
mouth. Mushroom-shaped knob to cover.
Each of the four sides has a relief of a shield of
arms supported by the lion and unicorn and
containing respectively a lion passant, a harp, a
lion rampant and three quatrefoils, all within
borders of key fret.

31 Teapot
Staffordshire, about 1745
Height 4½ in (11 cm)

Simple loop handle, spout and upright knob.
Coloured dark-brown on the outside, raised
stringing rubbed white. Interior white. Sprigged
ornaments in white applied. These include a
bird, fruit and flowers. There is a touch of
white slip on the brown handle as a thumb-rest.

32 Pickle-dish
Staffordshire, about 1745
Diameter 7 in (17.7 cm)

Composed of six small heart-shaped dishes with
moulded decoration. A rosette in the centre.

A nest of eight of these small heart-shaped
dishes is illustrated in Mountford, *Staffordshire
Salt-glazed Stoneware*, London, 1971, pl 105,
where they are attributed to Thomas and John
Wedgwood of the Big House, Burslem.

33 Arbour-group
Staffordshire, about 1745
Height 7¾ in (19.5 cm)

This group consists of a man and woman seated
beneath a tree with their arms encircling each
other. The group is uncoloured.

Other examples are illustrated in the Glaisher
Collection *Catalogue*, pl 54, no 803, and in the
Willett Collection *Catalogue*, no 1640. Examples
without the bocage are known. An example is
illustrated in 'The Incomparable Art *Catalogue*',
fig 155 (Greg Collection, Manchester).

34 Teapot
Staffordshire, about 1750
Height 3 in (7.6 cm)

This little teapot is of a depressed form with
simple knob, spout and loop handle. It is
decorated with swirls of solid agate in
brownish-black and grey.

35 Mug
Staffordshire, about 1750
Height 5 in (12.7 cm)

Reeded strap handle with pinched end. Slightly
flared base with moulding.
Decorated with a bird and flowers in
scratch-blue on white.

36 Figure of Chung-li Ch'üan, One of the Eight Taoist Immortals
Staffordshire, about 1750
Height 7½ in (19 cm)

The un-coloured figure stands with a fan in his right hand and a peach in his left. He wears an open wide-sleeved robe held at the waist by a cord. He stands on a mound base.

Similar examples are illustrated in The Burlington Fine Arts Club Exhibition *Catalogue*, pl xxxix, no 49, The Schreiber Collection *Catalogue*, vol 2, pl 16, no 92, and in an article by Frank Tilley, 'The Savour of Salt-glaze', *Antique Collector*, September/October 1949, fig 5. A Whieldon example is illustrated in the Schreiber Collection *Catalogue*, vol II, pl 36, no 266. A model in porcelain marked 'Bristoll' is illustrated in Barrett, *Worcester Porcelain*, fig 2A and in Sandon, *Worcester Porcelain*, fig 2.

37 Teapot
Littler-Wedgwood, Staffordshire, about 1750
Height 4¾ in (12 cm)

Globular. Crabstock handle and spout. Conical knob.
Covered with a blue glaze with thick opaque white enamel decoration of sprays of flowers. Knob with white stripes.

Illustrated in Arnold Mountford, *Staffordshire Salt-glazed Stoneware*, Frome and London, 1971, pl 174.

38 Figure, Mezzetin from the Italian Comedy
Staffordshire, about 1750
Height 4½ in (11.5 cm)

The figure wears a loose brown cap, blue-grey tunic with pink cloak, brown breeches. The mound base on which he stands is coloured green and grey. The figure with a tree-stump support is taken from the Meissen original modelled by Reinicke and Kaendler from a series of *Commedia dell'Arte* figures ordered for the Meissen factory by Johann Adolf II, Duke of Weissenfels and after Luigi Ricconboni's *Histoire du Théatre Italien* first published in 1728.
A very similar example is illustrated in the *Catalogue* of the Glaisher Collection, pl 42, fig F.

Mezzetino was a zanni or servant of the *Commedia dell'Arte* with many characteristics of Brighella or Scapino.

See colour plate III

39 Pair of Swans
Staffordshire, about 1750
Height 7½ in (19 cm) and 8 in (20.3 cm)

The swans have extended upright necks with
open beaks showing their tongues as though
hissing. Two small cygnets are appearing from
below the parent birds. They are resting on a
mound. Except for touches of blue on the legs
and beak the birds are white.

40 Teapot
Staffordshire, about 1750
Height 4½ in (11 cm)

Crabstock handle spout and loop knob all
enamelled dark-brown.
Flowers, vine-leaves, a bird and squirrel
enamelled in pink, blue, two greens and yellow
on a white ground.

See colour plate IV

41 Teapot
Staffordshire, about 1750
Height 3¾ in (19.5 cm)

Globular in shape with crabstock handle and
spout, mushroom knob. Green ground with
polychrome floral decoration reserved within
panels surrounded by a yellow border and
scrollwork.

42 White figure of an Owl
Staffordshire, about 1750
Height 8¼ in (21 cm)

43 Sauce-boat
Staffordshire, about 1755
Height 3¼ in (8.5 cm); length 7½ in (19 cm)

Scalloped edge and three claw feet. 'Hungry
Hound' handle with dark-blue slip eyes.
Moulded with snails, shells, and gnomes.

44 Sauce-boat
Staffordshire, probably Whieldon-Wedgwood,
about 1755
Length 7 in (18 cm)

Moulded with Wyverns and plants in relief.
Simple grooved handle with pinched end.

A block for this sauce-boat is in the Wedgwood
Museum at Barlaston and is illustrated in
Luxmore, *English Salt-glazed Earthenware*,
pl 68, no 21.

45 Teapot
Cockpit Hill, Derby, about 1765
Height 4½ in (11.5 cm)

Moulded as a basket of fruit with typical Derby strawberry pattern spout and scroll handle in imitation of Wedgwood but with a blunt end and no moulded leaves; flat knob.
The general ground colouring is pink enamel, the fruits are picked out in green, pink, yellow, and red.

A similar Cockpit Hill salt-glaze teapot is in the Schreiber Collection, II, 190.

46 Jug
Probably Staffordshire, about 1760
Height 6¾ in (17 cm)

The jug has a simple strap handle with pinched end and is painted in brilliant polychrome enamel colours with lovers embracing in a landscape. Possibly enamelled by the Leeds firm of Robinsons and Rhodes.

47 Jug
Staffordshire, about 1760
Height 9 in (23 cm)

The jug has a flat loop handle and beak-shaped
spout. It has a scratch-blue decoration of a
warrior with a spear and floral decoration,
otherwise it is white.

Lead-glazed Earthenware

48 Charger
Staffordshire slipware, second half of
17th century
Diameter 13 in (33 cm)

Decorated with a geometric design in two
shades of brown and cream-coloured spots on a
yellow glazed ground.

49 Charger
Thomas Toft, second half of 17th century
Diameter 18 in (46 cm)

Four crowned heads surrounding a central
uncrowned head in dark-brown slip on a yellow
glazed ground. Trellis border of dark-brown
and ochre.

Previously exhibited at Birmingham City
Museum and Art Gallery.

Illustrated in Ronald G. Cooper, *English
Slipware Dishes*, no 121.

A nearly similar charger is in the Philadelphia
Museum of Art.

50 Tyg
Probably Staffordshire, early 17th century
Height 6 in (15.2 cm); diameter at top 6 in (15.2 cm)

A dark-red body covered by a brownish-black glaze. It has three simple loop handles and three small ornamental handles.

51 Posset-pot
English, perhaps Essex, 1740–1749
Diameter 8¾ in (22.2 cm); height 5 in (12.7 cm)

Eight loop handles. Dark-brown lead glaze. Small stamped decorations and incised date and initials '174? 1B'.

52 Harvest-jug
Probably Sussex, first half of 19th century
Height 10¼ in (26 cm)

Small ridged loop handle. The upper part only
is glazed with a rich brown lead glaze.

For a similar jug see C. D. Brears, *The English
Country Pottery*, Newton Abbot, 1971, p 70.

53 Teapot
Staffordshire, Agate ware, about 1740
Height 6¼ in (16 cm)

A four-sided teapot with square pedestal base,
marbled with brown on deep cream and lead
glazed. Moulded with the figure of Admiral
Vernon; the royal coat-of-arms and the scene of
Porto Bello on the four panels.

Illustrated in Sandon, *Coffee-pots and Teapots*,
Edinburgh, 1973 and in Tilley, 'A Galaxy of
Teapots', *Antique Collector*, January 1970.

54 Teapot
Staffordshire, Astbury type, about 1740–1750
Height 3¾ in (8 cm)

This little teapot is of an unusual shape being low and having a rectangular base. Its general colour is chestnut red with a lead glaze. It has a simple loop handle and spout and a seal knob. It is decorated with cream-coloured applied decoration consisting of the royal coat-of-arms on either side.

Formerly in the Lomax and Cecil Sharp Collections.

55 Teapot
Probably Staffordshire, about 1755
Height 4½ in (11.5 cm)

Globular teapot of the so-called Astbury type with crabstock handle, spout and knob to cover, also applied decoration, which includes the liverbird on both sides in pale-cream and gold leaf, the rest in ochre.

Formerly in the Collection of T. M. Ragg, see ECC 1948 Exhibition *Catalogue*, no 54.

56 Teapot
Staffordshire, about 1750. Astbury-Whieldon
type.
Height 3⅞ in (19.5 cm)

Globular with black glaze. Crabstock handle,
spout and bird knob white. Applied vine
decoration also in white.

Formerly in the Stoller Collection.

57 Teapot
Staffordshire, about 1750
Height 3⅝ in (19.3 cm)

Globular teapot of so-called Astbury type with
rich ochre glaze. Crabstock spout and handle
and applied flowers decoration white splashed
with brown, yellow and blue glazes. Flattish
knob with steam vent in ochre.

Formerly in the Stoller Collection.

58 Jug
Black-glazed Earthenware, probably
Staffordshire, mid-18th century
Height 7⅝ in (19.5 cm)

The jug is thrown with a simple strap handle
with a pinched end.

59 Mug
Staffordshire, Astbury type, about 1750
Height 4¾ in (12 cm)

Glazed redware mug with simple strap handle
with pinched end decorated with central band of
combed cream-coloured slip. The same slip
forms a rim to the mug as well as a touch on
the handle.

60 Teapot
Wedgwood-Whieldon, about 1758
Height 4⅝ in (11.5 cm)

Crabstock handle and spout, upright flower
knob.
Coloured with splashes of green, blue and
brown glazes, the brown being mottled.

61 Punch-pot
Whieldon, middle of 18th century, possibly
within the Wedgwood-Whieldon partnership
period, 1754–1759
Height 6¼ in (15.7 cm)

Crabstock handle and spout, pierced button
knob with notched edge. Applied vining and
florettes.
Dappled grey background with touches of
brown, yellow and green on flowers.

Illustrated in Sally Mount, *The Price Guide to
18th Century English Pottery*, p 187.

62 Tile
Thomas Whieldon, about 1750
5 in square (12.7 cm)

Decorated with touches of green, brown and
yellow glazes. It has a green border. The subject
is the fable of the stork and the fox.

63 Group
Whieldon type, Staffordshire about 1750
Height 4½ in (11 cm)

The man and woman are seated on a rock with
their arms round each other.
Decorated with glazes of dark browns and
greens and traces of blue.

A white salt-glaze version of this group is
illustrated in the Burnap Collection of English
Pottery *Catalogue*, pl 340. The colour-glaze
version is illustrated in Sir Harold MacKintosh,
Early English Figure Pottery, pl 5, fig 10, and in
R. K. Price, *Whieldon and Ralph Wood Figures
and Toby Jugs*, pl XX, fig 97, also in Herbert
Read, *Staffordshire Pottery Figures*, pl 20.

64 Teapot
Whieldon, about 1756
Height 5 in (12.7 cm)

Globular teapot with crabstock handle, spout and twig knob to cover.
Coloured with glazes of purplish-grey, yellow, green and brown. Numerous applied details include the King of Prussia on both sides, Prussian eagle and emblems of war.

65 Figure of Cat
Staffordshire, about 1760
Height 6½ in (16.5 cm)

The cat is seated on a plinth ¾ in (4.5 cm) deep.
It is decorated with brown, yellow and grey glazes. Interior plain glazed creamware.

Formerly in the Wilfred Evill Collection.

66 A Stag and a Hind at Lodge, a Pair
Ralph Wood, about 1770
The stag length 6½ in (16.5 cm); the hind
length 6 in (15.2 cm); height 5 in (10.7 cm)

The general colour is dappled fawn, the
moulded mound on which they recline is green
and ochre. The interior is unglazed.

A similar pair is illustrated in R. K. Price,
*Whieldon and Ralph Wood Figures and Toby
Jugs*, pl XL, fig 79.

See colour plate V

**67 A Pair of Figures – A Sailor and his
Companion**
Ralph Wood, about 1770
Height of sailor 8 in (20.2 cm); height of sailor's
lass 8½ in (21.5 cm)

The sailor wears a green jacket and yellow
waistcoat, light brown trousers, black hat, scarf
and shoes and stands on a green rocky mound
base. His companion wears a white skirt, yellow
bodice and green overmantle and hat and also
stands on a rocky mound.

Similar pairs are illustrated in Mackintosh,
Early English Figure Pottery, figs 38, 39;
Herbert Read, *Staffordshire Pottery Figures*,
pl 35.

68 Figure of Admiral Van Tromp
Ralph Wood, about 1770
Height 10¾ in (27 cm)

The Admiral stands on a high pedestal base
with tree-stump support and is seen in the act
of drawing his sword. The base is decorated
with three oval portrait medallions in brown,
one at the front and one on either side. The
Admiral wears an aubergine tunic, green
breeches, dark-brown shoes and hat, all in
colour-glazes.

The figure is that of the famous Dutch Admiral
who fought many battles against Admiral Blake
of the British navy. He was very popular with
both friend and foe.

Similar figures of Van Tromp are illustrated in
Harold MacKintosh, *Early English Figure
Pottery*, no 84; R. K. Price, *Astbury, Whieldon
and Ralph Wood Figures and Toby Jugs*, no 21.

69 Teapot
Wedgwood-Whieldon partnership, about 1758
Height 3¾ in (9.5 cm)

Cream-coloured earthenware with cabbage-leaf spout scroll handle and twig knob to cover, moulded as a melon and coloured with green and yellow glazes.

Illustrated in H. Sandon, *Coffee-pots and Teapots*, Edinburgh, 1973, also in F. Tilley, 'A Galaxy of Teapots' *Antique Collector*, January 1970.

70 Teapot
Wedgwood-Whieldon partnership, about 1758
Height 4½ in (11 cm)

Cream-coloured earthenware with leaf-moulded spout, handle as a lamprey, flat flower knob, moulded as a pineapple and coloured with green and yellow glazes.

Illustrated by H. Sandon in *Coffee-pots and Teapots*, Edinburgh, 1973.

71 Tea-caddy
Cambrian Pottery, Swansea, 1771
Height 4¾ in (12 cm); width 4⅛ in (10.4 cm)

Straight sides with moulded bead and reel
borders at neck, shoulder and twice round
base. Colour-glazed horizontal bands of green,
yellow and purplish brown. 'When this you see
Rember (sic) mee all tho many Miles wee
Distance be Swansea March 9 1771' inscribed in
scratch-blue.

Illustrated in *ECC Trans*, vol 6, pt 3, 1967,
pl 73A, also in *Catalogue* of Swansea Pottery
Bicentenary Exhibition 1768–1968, item 4, pl 1.

Exhibited at Swansea Bi-centenary Exhibition,
Glyn Vivian Art Gallery, Swansea, 1968.

72 Coffee-pot
Melbourne about 1768
Height 9¼ in (23.5 cm)

Deep-cream. Bead and reel edging top and
bottom and on cover. Double reeded handle and
terminals, sherds of which were found on the
Melbourne site. Fluted spout with moulded
leaves at its base. Convolvulus flower-knob with
three leaves at its base, uncoloured.

Illustrated in Towner, *English Cream-coloured
Earthenware*, London, 1957, pl 28; *ECC Trans*,
vol 8, pt 1, 1971, pl 30.

Exhibited at the Kenwood 1958 Exhibition.

73 Covered Cream-bowl and Stand
Melbourne
Total height 9½ in (24 cm)

Deep-cream, twelve-sided with pierced openwork and green floral decoration in thick enamel in alternate panels; ring knob and two handles twisted as a rope with terminals characteristic of the Melbourne Pottery. Lower part of bowl with double walls.

74 Taper-stick
Melbourne, about 1765
Height 6¾ in (17.2 cm)

Deep-cream, derived from silver. Gadrooned edge and beading.
Enamel-painted with flower sprays in purple monochrome.

Illustrated in *ECC Trans*, vol 8, pt 1, 1971, pl 18.

Exhibited Derby Exhibition, Morley College, 1976.

The attribution to Melbourne is made on the grounds of colour, glaze, workmanship and painting.

75 Fruit-basket and Stand
Wedgwood, about 1770
Diameter of stand 9½ in (24 cm); diameter of
basket 7 in (17.7 cm); height of basket
3½ in (9 cm)

Deep cream, elaborately pierced and moulded.
Enamel painted in purple monochrome with
flowers in the style of James Bakewell.

The shape is as illustrated in Wedgwood's
original *Queensware Catalogue*, 1770.

76 Teapot
Probably Melbourne, about 1765
Height 4½ in (11 cm)

Straight sided with double-twisted handle and
spout with moulded lobes at the base, flower
knob, terminals applied to both handle and
knob, bead and reel moulding to top, bottom
and shoulder and on cover.
Painted in red enamel with an all-over scale
pattern. Flower-knob and terminals touched
with green, blue and yellow.
The Melbourne attribution is made largely on
the strength of the spout which is almost unique
but of which sherds were found on the
Melbourne site.

77 Teapot

Leeds Pottery, about 1771
Height 5 in (12.5 cm)

Deep-cream. Double rope handle with
terminals. Spout elaborately moulded with
foliage. Cover surmounted by a convolvulus
flower-knob. Straight sided with bead and reel
edging top, bottom and shoulder as well as on
the cover.
Enamel painted in red and black with a young
lady wearing a hat and carrying a page of music
seated by a tomb on which is inscribed 'Solitude
is my Choice'. On the reverse are buildings and
trees. Terminals painted with blue, yellow,
green and black. Painted by the Leeds firm of
J. Robinson.

Illustrated in Towner, *The Leeds Pottery*,
London, 1963, pl 16B, *ECC Trans*, vol 9, pt 2,
1974, pl 72.

78 Jug

Leeds Pottery, about 1772
Height 7 in (17.8 cm)

Deep-cream with bead and reel edging top and
bottom. Double reeded handle with terminals
and turned horizontal bands.
Enamel painted in black and red with the verse –

> 'When this you see
> Remember me
> Tho' many miles
> We distant be.'

set within a cartouche of painted scrollwork.
Terminals touched with blue, green and yellow
enamel.

Illustrated in *ECC Trans*, vol 9, pt 2, 1974,
pl 81.

79 Jug
Yorkshire, probably Leeds area, about 1770
Height 8¼ in (21 cm)

Deep-cream. Double handle with strawberry terminals, and leaves under the spout. Bead and reel edging top and bottom.

Enamel painted with a North country farmer carrying a stick with a ram's horn handle. On the reverse a farm house and cattle on the hills. Painted in red, black, blue, green and yellow. Inscribed 'Ed Clayton' in dark red. Painted by the Leeds firm of J. Robinson.

Illustrated in *ECC Trans*, vol. 9, pt 2, pls 74, 75.

See colour plate VI

80 Coffee-pot
Cockpit Hill, Derby, about 1765
Height 8½ in (21.5 cm)

Deep-cream. Strap-handle with pinched end,
tall, upright spout of usual coffee-pot pattern,
pierced mushroom knob.

Enamel painted with a large spray on each side,
containing a number of different flowers.
Scattered sprigs of cherries both on the pot and
cover. Colours used are red, rosy-purple, green,
yellow and blue.

81 Teapot
Cockpit Hill, Derby about 1765
Height 4 in (10.2 cm)

Deep-cream. Facetted handle and spout and
pierced button-knob.
Enamel painted in red monochrome with
flower-sprays within a cartouche of painted
scrollwork.

Exhibited at the Derby Exhibition, Morley
College, 1976.

The general shape, handle, spout and knob as
well as glaze conform exactly with marked and
dated Cockpit Hill pieces.

82 Plate
Mark: two nicks in the foot-ring
Melbourne, about 1770
Diameter 9½ in (24 cm)

Deep-cream, with a feather border consisting of
eight barbs with a space after the first three.
This conforms with sherds found on the
Melbourne site.
Transfer-printed in black with a Chinese woman
fishing. A child is seated beside her. Four
vignettes of exotic birds on the flange.

The fishing scene occurs in reverse on a
Liverpool tile in the Schreiber Collection II 25.

83 Coffee-pot
Mark: 'J. D.' incised
Probably Holbeck, Leeds, Joseph Dennison's
Pottery, about 1768
Height 10 in (25.4 cm)

Deep-cream. Double handle with terminals
(hitherto unrecorded), pearl-beading top and
bottom and on cover; cover surmounted by a
large convolvulus flower-knob and same
terminal, tall, upright spout of usual coffee-pot
pattern.
Enamel painted in red monochrome with a large
butterfly within a cartouche of painted
scrollwork. On the reverse is a seated man
playing the bag-pipes with a dog and flask
beside him. Terminals and flower-knob touched
with purple, green and yellow enamel. The
painting though not typical may have been
done by the Leeds firm of Robinson and
Rhodes.

Not hitherto recorded, exhibited or illustrated.
The Holbeck Pottery was advertised for sale in
1769 one year before the completion of the
Leeds Pottery in 1770.

84 Teapot
Leeds or perhaps Staffordshire, about 1770
Height 5 in (12.7 cm)

Deep-cream, globular with pearl-beading top
and bottom and on cover. A moulded band of
trellis at one time gilded, round the widest part
of the pot. Double handle joined at the base
with a pinched end, moulded fern pattern
spout. Although almost certainly Leeds, a
number of unglazed spouts of this pattern have
been recently excavated in Staffordshire. The
knob is mushroom shaped. Enamelled with
floral sprigs in black and red.

85 Plate
Mark: two nicks in foot-ring
Melbourne, about 1765
Diameter 10 in (25.4 cm)

Deep-cream. Royal shape edged with moulding
border derived from silver, sherds of which
were found on the site of the Melbourne
Pottery.
Enamel painted in green, purple, red and gold
over a transfer-print of the arms of Baronet
George Brydges Rodney. Rodney was created
Baronet in 1764 and Baron in 1782.

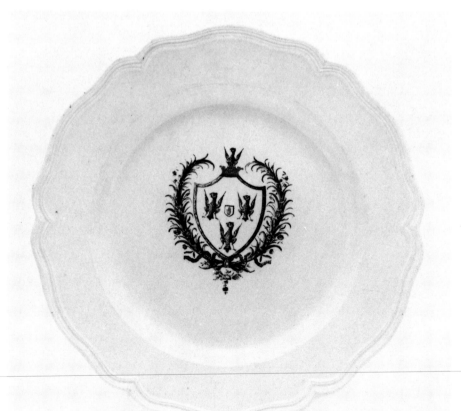

86   Punch-bowl
Probably Liverpool, about 1765
Diameter 10 in (25.5 cm); height 4 in (10 cm)

Deep-cream coloured.
Transfer-printed in black on the outside with
shepherd playing a flute seated under a tree
with a girl beside him stroking a dog. A castle is
in the background.
This print which is signed 'Rothwell Sculp' is
repeated on the interior. Also on the outside
repeated twice is 'Nancy Dawson dancing the
Hornpipe' derived and reversed from an
engraving in the *Ladies Amusement*, 1762, pl 32.

Illustrated in *ECC Trans*, vol 6, pt 3, pl 150C.
E. N. Stretton, Thomas Rothwell, 'Engraver
and Copper Plate Printer'; *Antique Collector*,
October 1971, p 201, fig 1.

87   Covered Vase
Cockpit Hill, Derby, about 1768
Height 10¾ in (27.3 cm)

Fairly deep cream colour. Ovoid with domed
cover.
Transfer-printed in black with an oriental lady
standing beside a bird-cage with a parrot above.
The reverse with peonies and rockwork. Sprays
of flowers on the shoulders, four butterflies on
the cover.

Illustrated in *Apollo*, January 1955, Knowles
Boney, 'A Ceramic Conundrum'; *ECC Trans*,
vol 6, pt 3, 1967, pl 187, Donald Towner, 'The
Cockpit Hill Pottery'; Geoffrey Wills, *English
Pottery and Porcelain*, 1969, p 156, fig 145;
Norman Stretton, *Antique Collecting*, July 1974;
'Some Rare Prints on 18th Century Cream
Ware', fig 6; Norman Stretton in 'A Ceramic
Conundrum: A Porcelain Tureen from Cockpit
Hill Derby', figs 3 and 4.

Exhibited at Morley College Exhibition of
Derbyshire Pottery and Porcelain, 1976.

Formerly in the Ernest Allman Collection.

88 Teapot
Mark: 'Wedgwood' impressed in lower-case
letters
Etruria, about 1774
Height 6 in (15.2 cm)

Pale-cream, globular with scale loop handle,
cauliflower spout and pierced ball knob.
Enamel painted by D. Rhodes & Co. in London
with a man seated under a tree playing the flute,
a house on the reverse and on the cover with
trees. The colours used are red, green, purple
and black. There are two workman's incised
marks underneath, one a scratched 'V' and the
other a small elipse.

Illustrated in Alison Kelly, *Wedgwood Ware*,
1970, p 32.

Exhibited at the Wedgwood Exhibition, The
Brewhouse Gallery, Eton College, March 1972.

89 Teapot
Wedgwood, about 1770
Height 5¼ in (13.4 cm)

Pale creamware, cauliflower spout, scroll handle
and pierced ball knob.
Enamel painted with a cross-banded decoration
in red, black, green, yellow and purple by the
London firm of D. Rhodes & Co.

90 Pairs of Figures of Street Musicians
Leeds Pottery, about 1785
Height 7½ in (19 cm)

A young man playing the tambourine and a young woman playing the hurdy-gurdy. They stand on square bases ⅞ in deep, hollow interiors with some of the corners thinned with a nick. Pale-cream, uncoloured.

A coloured pair marked LEEDS* POTTERY is in the Leeds Art Galleries collection.

Illustrated in Towner, *The Leeds Pottery*, London, 1963, pl 42A and B.

91 Coffee-pot
Leeds Pottery, about 1780
Height 6¼ in (16 cm)

Pale-cream with pearl-beading top and bottom
and two rows on cover. Conical shape.
Double-reeded handle with strawberry
terminals. The cover with grooved flower-knob
and typical Leeds terminal. Spout with moulded
fern decorations, uncoloured.

Illustrated in Towner, *The Leeds Pottery*, pl 22B.

92 Teapot
Melbourne, about 1772
Height 6 in (15.2 cm)

Pale-cream. Straight-sided with large
pearl-beading top, bottom, shoulder and cover.
Spout moulded with foliage springing from the
top. Handle, double grooved at the sides with
terminals in the form of roots. Convolvulus
flower-knob with three leaves at its base.
Enamel painted by a Derby painter with
Harlequin and Columbine on one side and a
Chinese figure on the reverse in red, green,
blue, yellow and black.

Illustrated in Towner, *English Cream-coloured
Earthenware*, London, 1957, pl 31B; *ECC
Trans*, vol 8, pt 1, 1971, pl 34A, B.

Exhibited at the Kenwood 1958 Exhibition of
Leeds Creamware.

93 Set of Four Figures Representing the Seasons
Neale & Co. Hanley, about 1780
Height of each figure 5½ in (14 cm), base 2¼ in (5.7 cm) square

Pale creamware. Each figure is impressed with the appropriate season that it represents – 'Spring', 'Summer', 'Autumn', 'Winter'. Enamelled in various colours. They stand on square bases with rococo scrollwork.

A similar set in the Glaisher Collection, Fitzwilliam Museum, Cambridge is illustrated in Towner, *English Cream-coloured Earthenware*, London, 1957, pl 94. One of these is impressed 'Neale & Co.'. There seems to be a difference in the 'Spring' of the two sets.

Illustrated in Godden, *Encyclopaedia of British Pottery and Porcelain*.

94 Two Screw-top Boxes
(a) Cockpit Hill, Derby, about 1770
Diameter 3 in (7.6 cm)

Pale-cream with gadrooned sides and edge to cover.
Enamel painted with a bird on the cover and flower spray on the base in purple, green, red, black and yellow. Purple sponged band round the side. The painting is by a well-known Derby hand.

(b) Wedgwood, about 1770
Diameter 3 in (7.6 cm)

Pale cream painted top and bottom with flower sprays in purple and red. Smaller sprays on the side. The painting is in the manner of James Bakewell.

Illustrated in Towner, *English Cream-coloured Earthenware*, London, 1957, col pl C.

Exhibited at the Kenwood 1958 Exhibition of Leeds Creamware.

95 Cup and Saucer
Leeds Pottery, about 1780
Height of cup 2 in (5 cm); diameter 3 in (7.6 cm); diameter of saucer 5⅛ in (13 cm)

Pale-cream with double-reeded handle and terminals.
Enamel painted with sprays of flowers in yellow, red, green and purple. Terminals touched with green and purple enamel.

Illustrated in Towner, *English Cream-coloured Earthenware*, London, 1957, pl 40B; Towner, *The Leeds Pottery*, London, 1963, pl 31 Bii.

Exhibited at the Kenwood 1958 Exhibition of Leeds Creamware.

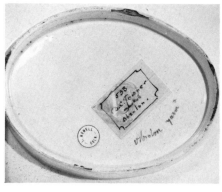

96 Dish

Shorthose or Davenport, signed underneath 'Absolon Yarm' in enamel, about 1800
Length 10½ in (26.5 cm)

Pale-cream. Painted by William Absolon with a river scene with boats, a tree and a castle in green, sepia and bluish grey enamel colours.

Illustrated in *ECC Trans*, vol 5, pt 1, pl 49, Kiddell, 'William Absolon, Junior, of Great Yarmouth'.

97 Punch-bowl

Liverpool, 1781
Diameter 8¾ in (22.2 cm)

Transfer-printed in black by Sadler and Green depicting Neptune, Venus and two pastoral scenes. On the inside within a black painted border is a print of a three-masted ship. The flags are touched with red and the sea with green. Below the ship is the inscription 'Solitude is my Choice Elizabeth Bouden 1781'.

98 Teapot
Wedgwood, about 1765
Height 5½ in (14 cm)

Deep-cream, globular with scroll handle and
cauliflower spout, the cover with pierced ball
knob.
Transfer-printed by Sadler at Liverpool in red
with 'The Minuet' on one side and 'Blind Man's
Buff' on the reverse. The cover with fruits,
flowers and insects.

Illustrated in *Connoisseur*, August 1976, Norman
Stretton, 'Liverpool Engravers and Their
Sources', p 266, fig 8.

The source of the print is from Bowles Drawing
Book 1757.

99 Jug
Probably Liverpool, about 1785
Height 9¾ in (24.8 cm)

Baluster shape with flat loop handle, ribbed at
the edges.
Enamelled on one side in red, blue, green,

yellow and black with a two-masted sailing ship
flying the English flag, inscribed below 'Success
to the Fly Joseph Swayne Master'. On the
reverse side a coat of arms transfer-printed in
black and touched with the same enamel
colours. Below is the motto 'Non Mihi Sed Deo
Et Regi'. The rim is painted with black feathery
scrolls.

Illustrated in 'People and Pots', Northern
Ceramic Society Exhibition *Catalogue*,
March 1976.

Previously exhibited at the Manchester
Museum.

100 Figure of a Horse
Leeds Pottery, about 1790
Height 16½ in (42 cm); length 14 in (35.5 cm)

The horse is cream with a dappled manganese
body, brown mane and tail and ochre trappings,
standing on a thin green-topped base with a
border of acanthus leaves. All colours are
mineral glazes.

101   Dessert-plate
Mark: 'WEDGWOOD' impressed
Between 1808 and 1811
Diameter 8¼ in (21 cm)

Decorated with botanical prints in underglaze
brown enamelled in iron-red and gilt, orange
coloured outside edge. Three species of
water-lily are depicted.
The 'Brown Water Lily' pattern is no 495 in
Wedgwood's first pattern book.

Illustrated in *ECC Trans*, vol 7, pt 2, 1969,
pl 142B, and in Alison Kelly, *Wedgwood Ware*,
1970, p 68.

102   Dish
Mark: 'SWANSEA' impressed and letter 'C'.
Cambrian Pottery, Swansea, about 1803
Length 10 in (25.5 cm)

Shaped edge with gilded rim and initials
R.J.R. in monogram.
Painted with a pigeon on a bough in natural
colours by William Weston Young. Inscribed in
blackish-brown enamel on the back are the
words 'Stock Pigeon'.

The painting is from Bewick's *British Birds*,
vol 1, p 278, where there is a woodcut of 'The
Wild Pigeon or Stock Dove'.

103 Mug
Cambrian Pottery, Swansea, about 1803
Height 2½ in (6.4 cm)

Enamelled in dark-brown, green and grey with
rocky landscapes on both sides with a figure,
gilded edges and letter 'G'.
Painted by William Weston Young (1776–1847).

Referred to in *Glamorgan Historian*, vol 5.
E. Jenkins, 'William Weston Young a
Glamorgan All-rounder'.

104 Coffee-pot
Cambrian Pottery, Swansea, about 1794
Height 10 in (25.5 cm)

Plain curved spout, loop handle and domed
cover with pierced ball knob.
Printed in underglaze-blue with the 'Elephant
and howdah' pattern on one side and the Prince
of Wales feathers on the other. The engravings
are by Thomas Rothwell.

Illustrated in *ECC Trans*, vol 6, pt 3,
pl 154A, B. Exhibited at the Morley College
Ceramic Circle Exhibition, 1974.

105 Plate
Mark: 'SPODE' over '31' impressed 'A' printed
in blue Spode
About 1816
Diameter 10 in (25.5 cm)

Printed in underglaze-blue with the 'Blue
Italian' pattern of ruins perhaps near Rome and
a border derived from a Chinese Imari pattern.

Exhibited at Frankfurt 1965, Oslo 1966, Royal
Academy 1970.

Illustrated in *ECC Trans*, vol 7, pt 2, 1969,
pl 138F in J. K. des Fontaines, 'Underglaze
Blue-printed Earthenware'.

106 Dish
Probably Staffordshire, about 1830
Length 17¼ in (44 cm); width 14¾ in (37.5 cm)

Transfer-printed in underglaze natural colours
with a view of Bolton Abbey and a blue-printed
border with flowers and butterflies.

107 Teapot
Elers, about 1690, Redware
Height 5¾ in (14.5 cm)

Globular standing on a high foot, large loop
handle and short straight spout, slightly domed
cover with pierced acorn knob. Blackish red in
colour with stamped reliefs of prunus blossom.
Original silver gilt chain from a mounting on
the handle to the knob then to the tip of the
spout with a small hinged cover. Underneath
are two seal marks impressed containing
imitation Chinese characters.

A similar teapot in the Victoria and Albert
Museum is illustrated in *ECC Trans*, vol 1,
no 2, 1934, pl 11B by W. B. Honey, 'Elers
Ware'.

108 Mug
Elers, about 1690, Redware
Height 3½ in (9 cm)

Globular with horizontally reeded neck, grooved
loop handle with small roll below, blackish red
with stamped reliefs of prunus blossom.

A similar mug but with silver mount to rim, in
the Victoria and Albert Museum is illustrated in
ECC Trans, vol 1, no 2, 1934, pl 1A,
W. B. Honey, 'Elers Ware'.

109 Coffee-pot
Mark: 'L.P.' impressed in a rectangle
Leeds Pottery, about 1780, Redware
Height 8¾ in (22.2 cm)

Pear-shaped with spreading foot, slightly domed
cover with pierced acorn knob. Scroll handle,
straight spout which narrows near the tip.
Engine-turned decoration.
This is the only known specimen of redware
having the L.P. mark which is sometimes found
on Leeds creamware.

110 Punch-pot
Mark: imitation Chinese seal mark impressed
English, about 1770, Redware
Height 7½ in (19 cm)

Globular with applied floral stamps, hunting
scene and Chinese figures. Crabstock handle.
Spout of a type sometimes found on Cockpit
Hill and Leeds creamware; pierced ball knob.

The square seal mark is illustrated in *ECC
Trans*, vol 5, pt 3, 1962, pl 150, fig X in
Robin Price, 'Some Groups of English Redware
of the Mid-eighteenth Century', pt II.

111 Black Basalt Teapot
Mark: 'E. Mayer'
Elijah Mayer of Hanley, about 1785,
Black Basalt
Height 4¾ in (12 cm)

Oval cylindrical body, with straight spout and
reeded handle with acanthus terminal. Cover
with knob as the widow with her barrel. Four
applied reliefs of children round the body.
Lower section is reeded and a *guilloche* border
round the shoulder and on the cover.

112 Teapot
Impressed mark: 'TURNER & CO'
Lane End, about 1785, Jasper Ware
Height 5¼ in (13.5 cm)

Pale-blue jasper with white reliefs of various
nymphs. Galleried rim with interlacing circles in
white. Loop handle with acanthus ending, also
on the spout. Cover with formal white foliage
and pierced onion shaped knob. Signature
impressed on the foot-ring.

113 Pair of Portrait Medallions
Impressed mark: 'Wedgwood & Bentley'
About 1775, Jasper Ware
Height 2 in (5.1 cm); width 1¾ in (4.5 cm)

Dark-blue dip with portraits of Queen Charlotte
and King George III (names impressed on the
front) in white relief. Framed in 18th century
wooden frames of black and gold.

Previously exhibited at Mint Museum of Art,
Charlotte, N.C., U.S.A., 1968.

114 Jug

Mark: 'TURNER' impressed

William and John Turner of Lane End, about 1794

Total height 9¼ in (23.5 cm)

The jug is of fine creamy-white stoneware. It has a fitted cover of Sheffield-plate with a domed top. The main decoration consists of a scene of archers in applied relief. Above this is a border design of vine leaves and grapes. The neck and upper part of the handle are painted in brown enamel.

A Turner jug and mug with the same archery scene are illustrated in Bevis Hillier, *The Turners of Lane End*, nos 15 and 17B.

115 Cream-jug
Mark: 'TURNER' impressed
John and William Turner of Lane End, about 1800
Height 4½ in (11.4 cm)

The jug is four sided and helmet shaped. It stands on four small bracket feet. Each side bears a medallion with a classical scene in white against a brown background.

A Turner jug of similar shape but in caneware is illustrated in Bevis Hillier, *The Turners of Lane End*, no 20C.

116 Jug
Mark: 'HERCULANEUM'
Liverpool, about 1805
Height 9½ in (24 cm)

This jug, which is stoneware with a solid
marbled slipcast body, is glazed inside. It has a

square shaped handle, the neck is horizontally
reeded, acanthus moulding round the base and
under spout, vine moulding round the base of
neck. The main moulded design consists of
rustic characters after Teniers. These are in
buff-colour.

A jug of similar type is illustrated in Alan
Smith, *Liverpool, Herculaneum Pottery*, London,
1970, pl 111.

Introduction

Porcelain Section

The Porcelain section of this Catalogue follows in the main a factory order arranged roughly in accordance with chronology, but groups the factories that used a soapstone body together and treats the hard-paste factories as a single entity. In addition, there are two sections devoted respectively to the wares of the uncertainly identified factories ('Girl-in-the-Swing', etc.) and to foreign hard-paste porcelains decorated in London. The bone china made in a number of different factories in the early years of the nineteenth century has been put together in a section at the end of this part of the Catalogue.

The selection of objects for the Exhibition among all those offered was a matter of no small difficulty, but every effort was made to choose not only pieces which were of high quality in themselves, but such as had special points of interest to recommend them. The final choice gives a cross-section of English porcelain production spanning the second half of the eighteenth and the first half of the nineteenth centuries which is of exceptional interest and variety. It is a curious fact that only one piece which was in the Circle's 1948 Commemorative Exhibition appears to have found a place in the present one. 1948 certainly had more to show in the way of the 'grander' Chelsea and Worcester wares, with Lord Fisher's great 'Maypole' group, the Bearsted vases, and the Dyson Perrins Worcester suites of blue-ground vases signed by O'Neale and Donaldson (all now to be seen in public collections); but 1977 has a more interesting selection of Liverpool and New Hall porcelains and some out-of-the-way rarities in many fields, and carries the story of English porcelain a little further than did the earlier exhibition, although it is only half the size.

The wares of the Chelsea factory are as well represented as they can be in a dozen examples, ranging from a Chinaman teacaddy of the triangle period, through a nice range of red-anchor pieces to a fine group of three Ranelagh Masqueraders of the gold-anchor phase of the factory's production. In the same context, reference should perhaps be made to the magnificent series of 'Girl-in-the-Swing' groups and the rare cream jug of the same origin listed further on in the Catalogue (nos 208–211). Bow is worthily represented by some notable figures from the hand of the 'Muses Modeller', a splendid clock-case commemorating the death of Handel and a good series of table wares, both those painted in underglaze-blue and those in enamels. The early period at Derby is well covered by some fine table-wares and by the magnificent white 'dry-edge' group of a Chinese man and woman symbolising the sense of Sight (no 148); the Chelsea-Derby period equally by figures of Camden, Wilkes and Conway, forming a significant political triad of the period.

Research since 1948 has revealed the existence of the factory at West Pans in Scotland as a continuation of that at Longton Hall in Staffordshire, and the earliest and latest wares in this series find their place in the present Exhibition. The fifteen exhibits of Worcester porcelain likewise range from the earliest, by way of one of the exceptionally rare figures, to a Chamberlain's piece of about 1810.

The Liverpool porcelain has already been alluded to but it may be pointed out that the wares of five different factories, mainly identified by the researches of Dr. Bernard Watney, can be seen in the present Exhibition and their points of difference studied. Caughley, Lowestoft, Pinxton and the later factories associated with William Billingsley are all represented here by a handful of objects apiece, whilst the hard-paste factories of Plymouth, Bristol and New

Hall make an interesting group ranging from a fine Plymouth polychrome enamelled tankard, through some characteristic Bristol figures attributable to Pierre Stephan, to an exceptional group of New Hall pieces, including a part tea service painted by Fidelle Duvivier (no 201).

The 1948 Exhibition contained no enamels. Since that date most of the discoveries in the field of English enamels have come from members of the Circle, and have been published in its *Transactions*. It therefore seemed appropriate to show a number of enamels in the present Exhibition, and the pieces selected cover most of the spectrum between the early productions of experimental character made even before the middle of the eighteenth century in Birmingham and London, through the work of the Battersea factory, to the products of the South Staffordshire workshops of the second half of the eighteenth century; also included are one or two pieces out of the mainstream, such as a putative Liverpool badge and a plaque painted by W. H. Craft.

R.J.C.

Chelsea Porcelain

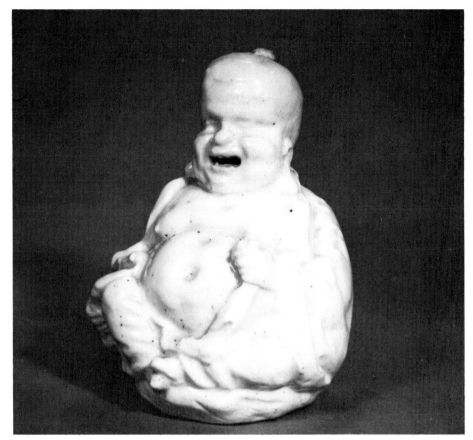

117 Incense-burner
Chelsea, about 1745–1749
Height 6 in (15.2 cm)

Formed as a squatting deity (*Pu T'ai Ho Shang*, god of Contentment), with protuberant belly, clutching his draperies with his left hand, and with his mouth open. The base is open and there is an aperture in the top of the head.

Illustrated in Arthur Lane, *English Porcelain Figures of the 18th Century*, London, 1961, pl 2A.

Doubtless based on a Chinese white figure from Fukien (see, eg, P. J. Donnelly, *Blanc de Chine*, London, 1969, pl 5B). Essentially the same model is used with the addition of a detachable hat, as a teapot (eg W. B. Honey, *Old English Porcelain*, London, 1948, pl 1E) or a tea-caddy (eg Y. Hackenbroch, *Chelsea and other English Porcelain . . . in the Irwin Untermyer Collection*, London, 1957, pp 12–13, fig 7, pl 2).

118 Teapot and Cover
Chelsea, about 1752
Height 5 in (12.7 cm)

Ovoid teapot with fluted body and cover, plain ribbed loop-handle and straight spout, the cover with piriform finial.
Painted in enamel-colours within lobed panels with 'harbour scenes' of people awaiting the arrival of sailing ships, similar smaller scenes on the cover. Scattered flowers and insects are painted on body, handle and spout.

See for the shape, B. Rackham, *Catalogue* of the Schreiber Collection, I, London, 1928, no 188.

See colour plate VIII

119 Teapot and Cover
Chelsea, about 1755
Height 5 in (13 cm)

Teapot and cover octagonal on plan, with
angular handle and straight spout, both of
square section.
Painted in enamel-colours with figure scenes
within oblong panels, one of a drunken peasant
mocked by his wife, the other of cattle and
sheep with a herdsman. Polychrome flowers and
insects on the cover and body of the pot.
The painting has been attributed to Jefferyes
Hamett O'Neale.

120 Plate
Chelsea, about 1755
Diameter 9¼ in (23.5 cm)

Plate with notched and lobed rim moulded in
relief with three rococo panels, separated by
leaves and trellis diaper.
Painted in enamel-colours in the panels with
pairs of lovers in Watteau style in landscapes,
and in the centre with one large and three
smaller sprays of flowers, with a pair of large
leaves. The back of the rim is overpainted with
yellow ground colour.

For the moulded design see ECC Exhibition
Catalogue, 1948, nos 230–231.

121 Plate
Mark: an anchor in red enamel
Chelsea, about 1755
Diameter 9¼ in (23.5 cm)

Plate with waved edge.
Painted in enamel-colours with a scene of three boys flying a kite, below which is rococo scrollwork in puce. Round the rim are sprays of flowers and leaves in polychrome.

Illustrated in Cyril Cook, 'The Art of Robert Hancock', *ECC Trans*, vol 3, pt 1, 1951, p 54 ff, pl 22C; F. Severne Mackenna, *Chelsea Porcelain, The Red Anchor Wares*, Leigh-on-Sea, 1951, pl 26.

The design is adapted from an engraving by J. Bachelet after H. Gravelot.

122 Plate
Mark: an anchor in red enamel inside the footrim
Chelsea, about 1755
Diameter 9¼ in (23.5 cm)

Plate with waved rim.
Painted in enamel-colours (two greens, lilac, orange, yellow) with outlining in purple, depicting in botanical style an orange and a spray of orange blossom.

123 Covered Box in the Form of an Apple
Mark: an anchor and '2' in red enamel on the box
Chelsea, about 1755
Height 4 in (10 cm); length 4 in (10 cm)

Naturalistically modelled and painted in enamel-colours with a stalk and three leaves, and a handle in the form of a codling moth caterpillar.

See (ed.) R. Blunt, *The Cheyne Book of Chelsea China and Pottery*, London, 1924, p 74, pl 15, nos 307–8.

The Chelsea Sale Catalogue for 10 March 1755, includes (Lot 48) 'four fine apples and 4 leaves, for desart'.

124 Bodkin Case
Chelsea, about 1755
Height 5⅛ in (13 cm)

Formed as a stick of broccoli and mounted in gilt metal.
Painted in enamel-colours, the details of the broccoli in green and purple, a spray of roses and leaves on the base in polychrome.

See John Austin, *Chelsea Porcelain at Williamsburg*, Williamsburg, 1977, no 100.

125 Figure of a Duck (originally one of a pair)
Mark: an anchor in relief on a raised pad
Chelsea, about 1750
Height 4½ in (11.5 cm)

The Duck stands on a gnarled tree-stump, preening under its right wing.
Painted in enamel-colours, the plumage blue, red, yellow, brown, puce and green, while the tree stump is painted with a patch of green and yellow 'moss' on one side.

See B. Rackham, *Catalogue* of the Schreiber Collection, I, London, 1928, no 145; Y. Hackenbroch, *Chelsea and other English Porcelain . . . in the Irwin Untermyer Collection*, London, 1957, pp 28–29, fig 19, pl 11.

The figure is taken from an engraving illustrating George Edwards, *Natural History of Uncommon Birds*, London, 1743–1747, vol II, pl 100.
The Chelsea Sale Catalogue for 10 March 1755, Lot 65, lists 'Four very fine DUCKS in different postures'.

From the Sanders Stephens Collection.

126 Figure of a Chinese Mask
Mark: an anchor in red enamel
Chelsea, about 1755
Height 6¾ in (17.2 cm)

The figure stands with left foot advanced, his right arm across his breast and his left hand behind his back, on a pad-base with applied flowers and leaves.
Painted in enamel-colours – yellow cap, black beard, lilac shoes, and polychrome flowers. Cloak, cap, tunic and breeches are edged with gold.

The Chelsea Sale Catalogue for 20 March 1755 lists (Lot 25): 'Three figures of an Italian doctor, a Chinese mask, and a beggar'. See also Kathryn C. Buhler, *English Porcelain Figures*, Museum of Fine Arts, Boston, fig 16.

Further examples of this figure are in the National Museum of Wales, Cardiff, and at Uppark House, near Petersfield.

127 Group of a Boy Riding on a Seal's Back
Chelsea, about 1755
Height 4½ in (11.5 cm); length 7 in (17.5 cm)

The boy sits astride the seal, his left hand on its head and his right holding a blue ribbon round its neck.
Enamel painted in natural colours.

One of a pair, the other being a girl on a dolphin.
F. Severne Mackenna, *Chelsea Porcelain: The Red Anchor Wares*, Leigh-on-Sea, 1951, pl 53–54; Chelsea China Exhibition, Royal Hospital Chelsea, 1951, *Catalogue* no 126.
See ECC Exhibition *Catalogue*, 1948, no 273 and B. Rackham, 'Red-Anchor Chelsea Figures at Woburn Abbey', *Old Furniture*, IV (1928), pp 110–113.

128 Three Figures of Ranelagh Masqueraders
Mark: a gold anchor
Chelsea, about 1760
Height 7⅞ in (20 cm) and 8¼ in (21 cm)

The figures consist of (1) a Dancing Man in a slouch hat, with left leg raised; (2) a Masked Soldier with gun, sword and powder-barrel under his arm; and (3) a Vivandière wearing a tricorn hat, a drum at her waist, and riding crop and carbine slung over her back. The mound-bases are decorated with rococo scrollwork and applied flowers and leaves.
Painted in enamel-colours (black, purple, turquoise, iron-red, yellow and mauve) for the costume and staffage, the scrollwork and other details picked out in gold.

Illustrated with one other of the set, Arthur Lane, *English Porcelain Figures of the 18th Century*, London, 1961, pl 25; see also (ed) R. Blunt, *The Cheyne Book*, London, 1924, pl 18; John Austin, *Chelsea Porcelain at Williamsburg*, Williamsburg, 1977, nos 130–139. Probably modelled by Joseph Willems, perhaps based on a print by C. Bowles after Maurer representing a masque held in Ranelagh Gardens on 24 May 1759, to celebrate the Prince of Wales's birthday.

From the Salting and the Sir B. Eckstein Collections, Sotheby's, 29th March, 1949.

See colour plate IX

Bow Porcelain

129 Tankard
Bow, about 1752
Height 3½ in (9 cm)

Cylindrical tankard with slightly spreading base
and ribbed loop handle.
Painted in underglaze-blue with the figures of a
woman and a Chinese boy in a canopied boat
watched by a woman with a parasol.

Illustrated by Bernard Watney, *English Blue and
White Porcelain*, London, 1963, pl 3A.

From the Aubrey J. Toppin Collection,
Sotheby's, 19th May 1970.

130 Jug
Bow, about 1750–1755
Height 5½ in (14 cm)

Jug oval on plan, with elaborately scrolled
handle. The upper surface of the foot is
gadrooned and the body of the jug is decorated
with four swags of flowers and leaves in relief.
Painted in enamel-colours with stylised flowers
and leaves.

131 Pair of Vases
Bow, about 1755
Height 10¾ in (27.5 cm)

Ovoid vase with spreading frilled foot and
narrow cylindrical neck with spreading rim.
Painted in underglaze-blue with birds (some
exotic) on leafy branches and among rushes.

Illustrated in Bernard Watney, *English Blue and
White Porcelain*, London, 1963, pl 9B; also
H. Tait, 'Bow' in (ed) R. J. Charleston, *English
Porcelain*, 1745–1850, London, 1965, pl 8A.

132 Clock or Watch Case
Mark: 'T⁰' impressed
Bow, dated 1759
Height 12¼ in (31 cm)

Clock-case in elaborate rococo style with
scrollwork picked out in puce and blue,
surmounted by the figure of *Father Time*

holding a scythe, two naked putti in relief
applied to the front angles of the case, and a
small figure of a cockerel below.
Painted in enamel-colours with sprays of flowers
and leaves on the sides and sheets of music
entitled 'Haymaker', 'a cantata', etc. The date
'5th November 1759' is inscribed on the case.

From the Mrs. Donald J. Morrison Collection,
Halifax, Nova Scotia, Sotheby's, 3rd April,
1973, Lot 194.

One of five surviving objects made at Bow to
commemorate the death of Handel, see Hugh
Tait, 'Handel and Bow', *Apollo*, July 1962,
pp 384–390.

**133   Tureen and Cover in the Form of a
         Duck**
Bow, about 1755
Height 3¼ in (8 cm); length 4½ in (11.5 cm)

Modelled in the form of a swimming duck with
head on one side.
Painted in enamel-colours, the feathers picked
out in sepia, puce and green, the head plumage
in russet brown and green, with bright yellow
beak.

Modelled after an engraving in George Edwards,
Natural History of Uncommon Birds, London,
1743–1747, III, pl 157, where the birds are
described as 'Little Brown and White Ducks',
(see Y. Hackenbroch, *Chelsea and other English
Porcelain . . . in the Irwin Untermyer Collection*,
London, 1957, p 29, fig 20, pl 10).

See colour plate X

134   Sweetmeat Dish
Bow, about 1760
Height 3½ in (9 cm); width 7 in (17.5 cm)

Scrolled rococo form inspired by contemporary
silver, the scrollwork picked out in puce, with
some green 'moss' patches.
Painted in enamel-colours on the inside with
sprays of flowers and leaves.

135   Pair of Figures of Henry Woodward as the Fine Gentleman and Kitty Clive as the Fine Lady in Garrick's Farce 'Lethe'
Bow, about 1750
Height of Henry Woodward, 10¼ in (26 cm); and Kitty Clive, 10 in (25.5 cm)

The actor stands by a pedestal wearing a tricorn hat, legs astride and hands thrust into the pockets of his breeches, the skirts of his coat tucked over his arms. The actress stands on a square base, wearing lace cap, elaborately frilled bodice and crinoline skirt, a spaniel under her right arm.

See Y. Hackenbroch, *Chelsea and other English Porcelain . . . in the Irwin Untermyer Collection,* London, 1957, pp 166–169, fig 241, pls 76–77.

Henry Woodward (1717–1777) and Kitty Clive (née Rafter, 1711–1785) played the 'Fine Gentleman' and the 'Fine Lady' in David Garrick's farce 'Lethe', the latter at least as early as 1740. The former model is based on an engraving by James McArdell after a painting by Francis Hayman, the latter on an engraving by Charles Mosley published in 1750 and based on the drawings by Thomas Worlidge. The Henry Woodward figure in the Untermyer Collection is dated 1750.

136 Group of Ki Mao Sao and Worshippers
Mark: 'E' in iron-red below base
Bow, about 1750
Height 6¾ in (17 cm); length 10¼ in (26 cm)

The goddess sits raised up in the centre with a
devotee on either side, one of whom she holds
by his pigtail. In the centre of the scrolled base
is a cartouche on which are inscribed
pseudo-Chinese characters in purplish-black.
Painted in enamel-colours (yellow, puce, green,
brown and black), the costumes with
sprig-patterns. The scrollwork of the base and
some other details are picked out in gold.

See H. Tait, *Porcelain*, London, 1962,
pl XXVI; Y. Hackenbroch, *Chelsea and other
English Porcelain . . . in the Irwin Untermyer
Collection*, London, 1957, p 171, fig 243, pl 80.
The model by the 'Muses Modeller' is taken
from an engraving by M. Aubert after Watteau,
entitled 'Idole de la Déesse KI MAO SAO dans
le Royaume de Mang au Pays de Laos'.

Aubrey J. Toppin, 'The Origin of some
Ceramic Designs', *ECC Trans*, vol 2, no 10,
1948, p 276, pl CII.

See colour plate XI

137 Pair of Figures of Virtues
Bow, about 1752
Height 8 in (20.5 cm)

Justice stands on a square plinth with left foot advanced, holding a sword (broken away) in her right hand and originally a pair of scales in her left. She wears a helmet and stands in front of a pile of books. Hope stands with crossed legs on a square plinth, leaning on an anchor (broken away).

Painted in enamel-colours (lavender, iron-red, yellow, blue and puce), the draperies with small sprigs of flowers and leaves. Sword hilt, helmet and hems picked out in gold.

By the 'Muses Modeller' – see A. J. Toppin, 'Some early Bow Muses', *Burlington Magazine*, LIV, 1929, pp 188–192; Arthur Lane, *English Porcelain Figures of the 18th Century*, London, 1961, p 87.

138 Pair of Figures of Lion and Lioness
Bow, about 1750–1755
Length 9 in (23 cm)

The Lion and Lioness face each other standing
on rockwork bases, their jaws open, the Lion's
tail coiled around his right leg, while that of the
Lioness rests on the ground.

139 Figure of a Girl
Bow, about 1765
Height 9¾ in (24.5 cm)

The figure (originally probably a sconce, the
candle-holder now missing), stands on a flat
scrolled base with left arm raised, her right arm
across her body touching the flowers in a basket
at her left side. The upper surface of the base is
decorated with applied flowers and leaves in
relief.
Painted in enamel-colours, the bodice yellow,
the kerchief puce, blue bustle with puce stripes,
and skirt decorated with sprays of flowers in
various colours. The base is picked out with
puce enamel and gilding.

Derby Porcelain

140 Basket

Derby, about 1756–1760

Height 4¾ in (12 cm); diameter 7⅞ in (20 cm); width between handles 8 in (20.5 cm)

Solid moulded basket with scalloped rim, the intersections of the 'basket' marked with fleurets picked out in yellow and puce; rope handles, each of two twisted stems with flower and leaf terminals, picked out in colours.
Painted inside in enamel-colours with a 'harbour-scene', ships and buildings in the background, figures with bales, etc., in the foreground. The sides of the basket inside are painted with four large, and a number of smaller, sprays of flowers and leaves.

141 Tureen and Cover
Derby, about 1756–1760
Length overall 14 in (35.5 cm)

Vertical-sided tureen on low footrim, oblong on
plan, with four narrow and four wide lobes,
having scrolled S-shaped handles on the long
axis picked out in turquoise and gold. Shallow
domed cover with handle in the form of a lobed
fruit with leaves.
Painted in enamel-colours at front and back
with domestic and exotic birds, at the ends with
butterflies, moths and other insects, on the
cover with an apple and a pair of cherries.
Probably painted by the 'Moth Painter'.

142 Bowl
Mark: (?) 'D' incised on base
Derby, about 1755
Height 2½ in (6.5 cm); width 3⅞ in (10 cm)

Bowl roughly square on plan, with indented
corners, decorated with applied sprigs of flowers
and leaves in relief.
Painted in enamel-colours with moths and other
insects by the 'Moth Painter'.

See Franklin A. Barrett and Arthur L. Thorpe,
Derby Porcelain, London, 1971, pp 8–9, pl 2.

143 Trinket-stand
Derby, about 1756–1760
Height 2⅛ in (5.5 cm); width 4½ in (11.5 cm)

Stand made in two parts – the top saucer-
shaped with waved rim and with a footring, on
a pedestal.
Painted in underglaze blue with small stylised
flower-sprays on the upper surface, and with
formal borders round the rim and foot.

Illustrated in Bernard Watney, *English Blue and
White Porcelain of the 18th Century*, London,
1973, pl 63C.
Exhibited at the Fitzwilliam Museum,
Cambridge (1967).

144 Perfume-burner in the Form of a Dovecote
Derby, about 1760
Height with cover 15⅜ in (39 cm)

Baluster-shaped dovecote with a 'roof' of scale-moulding, above and below which are holes for the pigeons, which come and go, modelled in full relief. The domed cover is surmounted by a bird with spread wings. The body of the dovecote is decorated with applied stems with leaves and flowers, all picked out in bright enamel-colours. At the base of the dovecote is a set of steps with a pointer to one side gazing at a quail on the other.
Painted in enamel-colours with moths, probably by the 'Moth Painter'. There are gilt flower-sprays between the pigeon-holes.

Illustrated in Franklin A. Barrett and Arthur L. Thorpe, *Derby Porcelain*, London, 1971, colour pl B. The shape, probably inspired by the red anchor Chelsea version of about 1755, is mentioned in Derby documents of a later date. (*ibid*, pp 151 and 173).

See colour plate XII

145 Chamber Candlestick
Derby, about 1775
Height 3⅜ in (6.5 cm); diameter 5¼ in (13.5 cm)

Candlestick formed of a lobed saucer with raised scroll border, fluted candle-holder with scalloped out-turned rim, and crabstock handle with leaf and flower terminals.
Painted in underglaze-blue with sprays of flowers and leaves, and insects.

Cf. (ed) R. Blunt, *The Cheyne Book*, London, 1924, no 66, pl 20, a pair of the same shape, identified as Chelsea.

146 Teapot and Cover

Mark: a crown over crossed batons and 'D', in puce on the base; '8' in puce inside the footrim; and 'O', impressed.
Derby, about 1790
Height 5¼ in (13 cm)

Globular pot on low foot, with plain loop handle, cover with ring-finial, and short spout with basal moulding.
Painted in enamel-colours within oval gold bordered panels with figures in a river landscape. Round the rim of the cover and the shoulder of the teapot run gold leaf-borders.

The painting has been attributed to Zachariah Boreman.

147 Sauce-tureen, Cover and Stand

Marks: crown over crossed batons, six dots and 'D'; also '343', all in blue enamel
Derby, about 1790
Width of stand 9¼ in (23.5 cm); height overall 6½ in (16.5 cm)

Boat-shaped tureen with pointed oval stand, and pointed handles on the long axis. The shallow domed cover has a ring handle formed of two joined stems.
Painted in enamel-colours with named landscapes within gilt oval panels – 'Near Woolwich' and 'Southampton': on the stand, 'Wingfield Manor Derbyshire'. Tureen, stand and cover are edged with a broad band of green, within which are gilt formal borders.

From the Col R. J. L. Ogilby Collection, sold Sotheby's, 21 July, 1964, lot 71 (ill).

The remaining parts of the service bore views in Great Britain and Italy. The painting is attributed to Zachariah Boreman.

148 Group Representing 'Sight'
Derby, about 1750–1754
Height 7½ in (19 cm)

A Chinese woman and a man sit on a rockwork
base, she with her left arm raised, he holding a
bottle in his right hand.

From a set of the Senses, perhaps modelled by
Andrew Planché – see Arthur Lane, *English
Porcelain Figures of the 18th century*, London,
1961, pp 98–99. See also Mrs. Donald
MacAlister, 'The Early Work of Planché and
Duesbury', *EPC Trans*, no II, 1929, pl XIII,
where is illustrated the original model from
which the head of the Chinese woman was
taken.

Cf. Y. Hackenbroch, *Chelsea and other English
Porcelain . . . in the Irwin Untermyer Collection*,
London, 1957, pp 197–198, fig 269, pl 100.

149 Pair of Figures, General Henry Seymour Conway and John Wilkes
Derby, about 1770–1775
Height 12⅝ in (32 cm)

Conway stands with his left hand on a cannon, his right on his hip, a *putto* at his feet supporting a shield with a Moor's head, his family's crest.
Wilkes stands with his left hand on his hip, his right on scrolls inscribed 'MAGNA CARTA' and 'BILL OF RIGHTS', a *putto* at his feet holding a book inscribed 'LOKC(sic) ON GOVT'. The scrolls are on a square pedestal inscribed in gold 'INO WILKES ESQ'.
Painted in enamel-colours and gilt, the scrolled bases picked out in turquoise enamel and gold.

Cf. Arthur Lane, *English Porcelain Figures of the 18th Century*, London, 1961, p 106; B. Rackham, *Catalogue* of the Schreiber Collection, I, London, 1928, nos 362 and A, pl 35; Franklin A. Barrett and Arthur L. Thorpe, *Derby Porcelain*, London, 1971, p 40, pl D.
John Wilkes first came into prominence with his libel on George III, published in 1763. General

Conway had defended him in 1764, and had been dismissed from his appointments in consequence. (See also no 150.)
These models were probably the work of Pierre Stephan.

150 Figure of Lord Camden
Derby, about 1770–1775
Height 12½ in (32 cm)

The Lord Chancellor stands on a marbled plinth-base, with his right hand on his breast, his left leaning on a book supported on a column embossed with a figure of Justice. He wears scarlet robes with ermine collar and cuffs, and a gold chain of office.
Painted in enamel-colours and gilt.

Cf. Arthur Lane, *English Porcelain Figures of the 18th Century*, London, 1961, p 106, pl 72. An example in the Fisher Collection was marked with the gold anchor – see (ed) R. Blunt, *The Cheyne Book of Chelsea China and Pottery*, London, 1924, no 241, pl 19.

The Rt. Hon. Sir Charles Pratt, as Chief Justice of the Court of Common Pleas, had in 1763 decided that the arrest of John Wilkes (see no 149) was illegal. He became the first Baron Camden in 1765 and Lord Chancellor in 1766. The porcelain figure is based on an engraving by S. F. Ravenet after the portrait by Sir Joshua Reynolds.

151 Figure of a Shepherd Playing the Flute
Marks: 'No 369' and a star, incised.
Derby, about 1790–1795
Height 10¼ in (26 cm)

Biscuit Porcelain. The boy stands on a circular
plinth, his legs crossed, leaning on a tree-stump.
On the plinth is a recumbent sheep and flowers
and leaves applied in relief.
The figure is shown in the Derby list with its
companion as: 'Shepherd and Shepherdess'.
(J. Haslem, *The Old Derby China Factory*,
London, 1876, p 178.)
The figure, modelled by J. J. Spengler, is a
clothed version of the 'Capitoline Faun'.
The star mark is identified as that used by the
'repairer' Isaac Farnsworth.

152 Pair of Pickle-trays
Perhaps Derby (Cockpit Hill), about 1760
Length 7¼ in (18.5 cm) and 7⅜ in (18.8 cm)

Shell-shaped dishes with deeply indented
crimped borders, standing each on three helical
shell-like feet.
Painted in underglaze-blue with a large spray
and smaller sprigs of flowers and leaves, the
border picked out in blue.

Exhibited at the Morley College Exhibition of
Derby Wares, 1976.

Longton Hall Porcelain

153 Leaf-dish
Longton Hall, about 1753
Length 8⅞ in (22.5 cm)
Lobed leaf-form with scalloped edge, the handle formed of two twigs intertwined.
Painted in enamel-colours with a rock in Chinese style and with sprays of flowers and leaves.

154 Sauce-boat
Mark: a saltire cross incised on the base
Longton Hall, about 1755
Height 5¼ in (13.5 cm); length 8½ in (21.5 cm)

Boat-shaped with tall pouring-spout and elaborate scrolled handle. The body is modelled with floral and leaf-sprays (differing on the two sides) and scrollwork below handle and lip. Painted in enamel-colours with floral sprays in 'salt-glaze' style.

From the Arthur Hurst and Michael Moseley Collections – see *ECC Trans*, vol 2, no 9, 1946, p 231, pl LXXIV B. Cf. Bernard Watney, *Longton Hall Porcelain*, London, 1957, pl 25B.

155 Guglet
Longton Hall, about 1755–1758
Height 10⅜ in (26.5 cm)

Globular-bodied bottle with swelling in the
neck.
Painted in under-glaze blue with
chrysanthemum, bamboo, etc. in Chinese style,
with formal diaper borders round the base and
the swelling of the neck.

156 Plate
West Pans (William Littler's factory), about 1766
Diameter 6 in (15.2 cm)

Small plate with scalloped rim and flat base.
Painted in enamel-colours with a bird on a
Chinese fence, a plant growing from rocks, a
butterfly, and flower-sprigs, all within a border
of 'Littler's blue'.

Illustrated in Bernard Watney, *Longton Hall
Porcelain*, London, 1957, pl 14; see Arthur
Lane, 'William Littler of Longton Hall and
West Pans, Scotland', *ECC Trans*, vol 5, pt 2,
1961, pp 82–94.

From the Rev. C. J. Sharp Collection.

157   Figure of Cupid at Vulcan's Forge
Longton Hall, about 1750–1752
Height 7¼ in (18.5 cm)

Cupid stands with his left arm resting on a
scrolled two-tier plinth representing the forge.
The base and figure are decorated with applied
flowers and leaves in relief.

Illustrated in Bernard Watney, *Longton Hall
Porcelain*, London, 1957, pl 2A; cf. also Watney
in (ed) R. J. Charleston, *English Porcelain
1745–1850*, London, 1965, p 74, pl 23A.

This piece belongs to the 'Snowman' group of
Longton Hall figures.

**158   Figure of an Infant Artist, symbolising
'Painting'**
Longton Hall, about 1755
Height 5⅜ in (8.5 cm)

The *putto* stands, palette in hand, with right
hand raised and head turned to his left to look
at a canvas resting on a tree-stump.
Painted in enamel-colours.

Cf. Bernard Watney, *Longton Hall Porcelain*,
London, 1957, p 38, pl 51.

This figure may originally have belonged to a
set of *The Liberal Arts*, or *Arts and Sciences*.

159 Figure, perhaps David Garrick
Longton Hall, about 1755
Height 7½ in (19 cm)

The actor stands with his left hand on his
breast, his right hand resting on an open book
supported on a plinth decorated in relief with a
theatrical trophy.

Cf. the coloured example illustrated in
B. Rackham, *Catalogue* of the Schreiber
Collection, I, London, 1928, no 431, pl 50,
where the actor holds a scroll inscribed with
words from *The Tempest*. See also ECC
Exhibition *Catalogue*, 1948, no 357 (Fisher
Collection).

Lund's Bristol and Worcester Porcelain

160 Tankard
Bristol (Benjamin Lund's factory), about 1750
Height 6¼ in (16 cm)

Cylindrical mug with spreading base and bold silver-shape handle picked out in blue scrollwork.
Painted in underglaze-blue with a Chinese landscape.

Illustrated in Bernard Watney, *English Blue and White Porcelain of the 18th Century*, London, 1973, pl 22A.

Exhibited at the Fitzwilliam Museum, Cambridge (1967).

161 Funnel
Bristol (Benjamin Lund's factory) or Worcester, about 1752
Height 5⅛ in (13 cm); diameter 4¾ in (12 cm)
Conical funnel of concave profile.
Painted in enamel-colours with the figure of a Chinese woman holding a blue fan, standing between a fir-tree and a group of shrubs. Round the rim inside is a border of eight panels, four in green diaper alternating with four enclosing half flower-heads.

Cf. H. R. Marshall, *Coloured Worcester Porcelain of the First Period*, Newport, 1954, pl 2, no 38; Franklin A. Barrett, *Worcester Porcelain and Lund's Bristol*, London, 1953, pl 8A; *Country Life*, 15 July 1976, p 150, fig 2.

162 Plate
Mark: three-character imitation Chinese mark
within a double ring, in underglaze-blue.
Worcester, about 1752.
Diameter 9⅜ in (23.8 cm)

Deep plate with slightly convex rim, and
recessed base.
Painted in underglaze-blue with a bird in a
flowering tree-peony, a fence and rocks: on the
rim, panels enclosing pomegranates and leafy
branches, on a diaper ground. On the reverse,
three of the Chinese 'precious objects'.

Illustrated in Bernard Watney, *English Blue and
White Porcelain of the 18th Century*, London,
1973, pl 25C.

163 Coffee-pot and Cover
Worcester, about 1754–1755
Height 6¾ in (17 cm)

Pear-shaped pot with scroll-handle and
umbrella-shaped knob.
Painted in enamel-colours with a cock pheasant
on a rock with flowering prunus, looking down
at a hen pheasant.

164 Guglet and Basin
Worcester, about 1755
Height of guglet 9⅝ in (24.5 cm); diameter of
bowl 9⅝ in (24.5 cm)

Guglet of bottle form with 'onion' mouth,
standing in a basin with over-turned rim.
Painted in enamel-colours with an exotic
pheasant-like bird on a tree, threatening a snail,
together with a length of Chinese fencing, and a
rock-formation.

See ECC *Catalogue of First Period Worcester
Porcelain 1751–1783*, London, 1951, no 84;
H. R. Marshall, *Coloured Worcester Porcelain of
the First Period*, Newport, 1954, pl 5. The same
theme of decoration is found on a 'scratch-cross'
tankard dated 1754 – see H. E. Rhodes,
'Inscribed and dated 'Scratch-Cross Pieces',
EPC Trans, III, 1931, pp 82–83.

165 Bowl
Worcester, about 1756
Height 3 in (7.5 cm); diameter 6 in (15 cm)

Hemispherical bowl on tallish wedge-shaped foot.
Painted in underglaze-blue with a continuous river-scene including a ship drawn up at a quay, with ruins and a tree: inside, a small scene with a man fishing.

Illustrated in Francis Burrell, 'Some Less Common Decoration on Worcester Porcelain', *ECC Trans*, vol 6, pt 1, 1965, p 9, pls 13B and 14; Bernard Watney, *English Blue and White Porcelain of the 18th Century*, London, 1973, pl 33C.

166 Sauce-boat
Worcester, about 1755
Height 4½ in (11.5 cm); length 8¾ in (22.2 cm)

Leaf-shaped boat moulded with horizontal rows of short overlapping (?) artichoke-leaves, with rosettes applied at the tips. Twisted stalk-handle with overlapping larger ribbed leaves extending from the base terminal, and pouring-lip decorated with similar overlapping leaves.
A hitherto unrecorded variant of the normal Worcester leaf sauce-boat

167 Dry Mustard-pot

Worcester, about 1755–1760
Height 4¾ in (9.5 cm); diameter of rim 1⅝ in (4 cm)

Pot of inverted baluster shape on pedestal foot, with high domed cover surmounted by a slightly pointed hemispherical knob.
Transfer-printed in black outline painted over in enamel-colours (blue, purple, green, yellow, iron-red, and pinkish-beige) with the 'Red Cow' design – a Chinese boy standing by rocks, to the right of which are two cows overpainted in red, and two Chinese figures, one a lady with a basket, the other a boy with a (?) parasol under his arm: on the cover, three insects.

Illustrated in G. Wills, *English Pottery and Porcelain*, Guinness Signature Series, London, 1969, fig 235; cf. H. R. Marshall, *Coloured Worcester Porcelain of the First Period*, Newport, 1954, pl 3, nos 50, 55, 57, for the shape; pl 9, no 164 for the design.

168 Teapot and Cover

Marks: crossed swords and '9', in underglaze-blue.
Worcester, painted in the London workshop of James Giles, about 1759.
Height 6½ in (16.5 cm)

Ovoid teapot with low domed cover surmounted by flower-finial, double interlaced handle with flower-terminals, and curved spout with basal moulding.
Painted in enamel-colours and gilt, with the arms of Currer of Kildwick, supported by *putti*, and the crest of Richardson of Bierley on the reverse. On the body and cover are sprays of flowers and leaves.

Illustrated and discussed in H. R. Marshall, 'Armorial Worcester Porcelain', *ECC Trans*, vol 2, no 9, 1946, p 207, pl LXVIII D.

Exhibited in the ECC *Catalogue of First Period Worcester Porcelain*, 1951, no 757.

Probably made for John Richardson, who succeeded to the Kildwick Estates in 1759 and assumed the name and arms of Currer.

169 Jug
Worcester, about 1760
Height 7⅞ in (20 cm)

Globular jug with cylindrical neck, the body
with 'cabbage-leaf' moulding, and handle with
small thumb-piece and acanthus-leaf moulding
at its lower end.
Painted in enamel-colours with figures in the
style of N. van Berchem, of a peasant on a
horse, with a girl to his left and sheep to his
right, ruins in the background. At the back and
round the rim, flower-sprays in puce
monochrome.

Cf. Franklin A. Barrett, *Worcester Porcelain and
Lund's Bristol*, London, 1953, pl 16.

See colour plate XIII

170 Teapot and Cover
Worcester, about 1760
Height, 4½ in (11.5 cm)

Barrel-shaped teapot, with horizontal reeding at
top and bottom, plain loop-handle and slightly
curved spout, the flat cover with flower-finial.
Painted in enamel-colours with formalised
flowers, leaves and insects, between areas of
yellow ground.

A similar teapot is in the Dyson Perrins
Collection, Royal Worcester Porcelain Company
Museum. See H. R. Marshall, *Coloured
Worcester Porcelain of the First Period*, Newport,
1954, pl 30, no 663.

171 Bowl

Worcester, about 1760
Height 3 in (7.5 cm); diameter 6 in (15 cm)
Roughly hemispherical bowl on tallish
wedge-shaped footrim.
Transfer-printed over-glaze in black with
Britannia in the centre, and to her right three
boys donning seamen's clothes, inscribed:
'Marine Society'; to her left, a group of a widow
and boys led towards her by a female figure
(Patriotism), with ribbon inscribed: 'For the
Service of our Country'. On the reverse is a
sea-battle, and in the centre inside a
bust-portrait of George II.

Illustrated in S. Hanscombe, *Northern Ceramic
Society Journal*, 1, 1972–1973, pp 13–17,
pls 1A–B, 2A–B; Cyril Cook, *Supplement to the
Life and Work of Robert Hancock*, Tonbridge,
1955, item 143; G. W. Capell, 'Some
unrecorded or rare transfer-printed pieces',
Connoisseur, December, 1953, p 168, figs IV,
IX, and X.

Exhibited at the Northern Ceramic Society
Exhibition, Leeds, 1974, no 111.

The Marine Society print was designed by
Samuel Wale and engraved by T. Major for the
Society: it appears as the frontispiece to *A Letter
from a Member of the Marine Society . . . with
respect to the Sea Service*, published by Jonas
Hanway (1st ed 1757, 2nd ed 1758).
The George II print was adapted by Robert
Hancock from a portrait by Thomas Worlidge
(Cyril Cook, *The Life and Work of Robert
Hancock*, London, 1948, item 52) and the
Worcester version of the Marine Society print
has also been attributed to him by Cook.

172 Bowl

Worcester, about 1760–1765
Height, 2⅞ in (7.2 cm); diameter 6 in (15 cm)

Hemispherical bowl on tallish footrim, with
six-lobed rim and six vertical grooves in the
sides. The rim is decorated with a band of
moulded ornament formed of half-fleurets
placed alternately up and down.
Painted in black enamel ('pencilled') with three
sprays of flowers and leaves and a butterfly. The
border inside is composed of four peony-blooms
in gold over-painted in red enamel, joined by
outlined flowers and leaves.

Cf. R. L. Hobson, *Worcester Porcelain*, London,
1910, pl LVII, 1. A spoon-tray in the Broderip
Gift at the Victoria and Albert Museum
(C 1345, 1924) has the same moulded pattern.

173 Figure of a Gardener
Mark: '8' in iron-red under the base.
Worcester, about 1770
Height 8¾ in (22 cm)

The Gardener stands in an elaborate arbour
with his spade in his left hand, a flowerpot
painted with gold flower-sprays in his right, on
a four-footed scrolled base picked out in
turquoise-green and gold.

Originally one of a pair of sconces, the
candle-holder missing. For the complementary
figure of a 'Gardener's Companion' see Franklin
A. Barrett, *Worcester Porcelain and Lund's
Bristol*, London, 1953, pl 87B. Cf. also Arthur
Lane, *English Porcelain Figures of the 18th
Century*, London, 1961, p 121, pl 87.

174 Cabinet Cup, Cover and Stand
Mark: 'Chamberlain's Worcester' in gold on the
cup and in red enamel on the cover
Worcester (Robert Chamberlain's factory),
about 1820
Height overall 4⅞ in (12.5 cm); width 5⅛ in
(13 cm); diameter of stand 5⅝ in (14.2 cm)

Straight-sided cup with opposed ring-handles,
low domed cover having a ring-handle formed
of overlapping leaf-forms, and stand with deep
central well.
Painted in enamel-colours with a scene of two
lovers, the man inscribing the bark of a tree,
within a panel with truncated corners. The
reverse, the cover and the stand are decorated
with a salmon-pink ground enlivened with
formal gilt designs.

The figural design, described as 'Love' in gold
letters under the base of the cup, is taken from
a painting representing Angelica and Medoro by
Angelica Kauffmann (B. Rackham, *Catalogue of
the Herbert Allen Collection*, London, 1917,
no 104). The painting is almost certainly by
Thomas Baxter.

Liverpool Porcelain

175 Jar and Cover
Marks: pseudo-Chinese characters inside cover and base, in underglaze-blue.
Liverpool (William Reid's factory), about 1758
Height with cover 9¼ in (23.5 cm)

Baluster-shaped vase with collar-neck and low domed cover surmounted by a knob-finial (the point broken off).
Painted in underglaze-blue with Chinese river-scenes, including a sampan, figures crossing a bridge, pagodas and other buildings, rocks, and trees; round the shoulder and above the foot, diaper-borders interrupted by oval panels enclosing flowering plants. The cover is similarly decorated.

Illustrated in (ed) R. J. Charleston, *English Porcelain, 1745–1850*, London, 1965, pl 38B.

Exhibited at the Fitzwilliam Museum, Cambridge (1967).

176 Figure of Minerva
Liverpool (Samuel Gilbody's factory), about
1755–1761
Height 5¾ in (14.5 cm)

The helmeted goddess stands with right hand
raised (probably originally holding a spear), and
left hand supporting her shield with the
gorgoneion, on a low mound-base decorated
with applied flowers and leaves.
Painted in enamel-colours (blue, rose-pink,
iron-red, green and yellow) with sprigs of
flowers and leaves outlined in black.

Illustrated in *ECC Trans*, vol 8, pt 2, 1972,
pp 229–230, pl 188.

The model resembles one made at Derby in
differing sizes and over a long period.

177 Mug
Liverpool (Samuel Gilbody's factory), about
1755–1761, probably 1757
Height 3½ in (9 cm)

Slightly tapering cylindrical mug with
elaborated silver-shape handle (cf. no 178).
Transfer-printed in black with a portrait of
Frederick the Great, inscribed: 'Fred.yᵉ IIIᵈ
KING OF PRUSSIA Elector of Brandenbourg',
within a rococo cartouche. The print, which has
been cut down to fit the mug, is signed:
'Gilbody Maker' 'Evans Sct'.

Cf. Bernard Watney, 'Four Groups of Porcelain,
possibly Liverpool', *ECC Trans*, vol 4, pt 5,
1959, pl 12A (a Worcester mug showing the
same transfer in its entirety).

Jeremiah Evans was a Liverpool engraver who
worked for John Sadler.

178 Mug

Liverpool (Samuel Gilbody's factory), about 1755–1761
Height 3½ in (9 cm)

Slightly tapering cylindrical mug with elaborate silver-shape handle (cf. no 177).
Painted in enamel-colours with one large and three smaller sprays of flowers and leaves, in orange-yellow, green, red-brown, pink and purple.

Illustrated in Bernard Watney, 'Four Groups of Porcelain, possibly Liverpool', *ECC Trans*, vol 4, pt 5, 1959, pl 13D; see also Bernard Watney and Alan Smith, 'Samuel Gilbody – Some Recent Finds at Liverpool', *ibid*, 7 pt 2, 1969, pp 100–107, pl 103C.

179 Plate

Liverpool (William Ball's factory), about 1755–1765
Diameter 9⅜ in (23.7 cm)

Transfer-printed in mainly purplish-black outline, filled in with enamel-colours (puce, yellow, blue, iron-red and green), with a variety of floral sprays and sprigs, and insects.

Cf. Newman Neild, 'Early Polychrome Transfer on Porcelain', *ECC Trans*, vol 1, no 3, 1935, pp 71–72; Frank Tilley, 'The so-called Polychrome Printing', *The Antique Collector*, September – October, 1946, pp 183–186.

180 Plate

Liverpool (William Ball's factory), about
1755–1765
Diameter 8⅞ in (22.5 cm)

Painted in underglaze-blue with, in the centre, a
stag and hind beside a tree and rocks; on the
rim, three landscape vignettes, with trees, rocks
and a temple in Chinese style.

Illustrated in Bernard Watney, *English Blue and
White Porcelain of the 18th Century*, London,
1973, pl 49A.

181 Flower-pot

Liverpool (William Ball's factory), about
1760–1765
Height 3⅝ in (9.5 cm); diameter 4¾ in (12 cm)

Flower-pot with thickened rim, applied
ring-handles, and hole in the base.
Painted in underglaze-blue with a Chinaman
seated under a tree holding a fan, this design
being repeated on the reverse. Below the rim
outside runs a diaper border.

182 Vase and Cover
Liverpool (William Ball's factory), about
1755–1765
Height with cover 25½ in (65 cm)

Baluster-vase with collar-neck and domed
flanged cover with pear-shaped finial.
Painted in underglaze-blue with a Chinaman
tending a tea-kettle over a brazier, while a boy

in the foreground dances beside an overturned
stool; on the reverse, a Chinaman hauls a
sampan, with buildings, trees and rocks in the
background. Round the shoulder, a diaper
border on which are reserved scrolled rococo
cartouches enclosing small landscapes,
flower-sprays, etc. Round the cover runs a
continuous Chinese landscape with boats on
water, buildings and trees on rocky islands. A

border similar to that on the vase encircles the
top of the cover.

Illustrated in B. Watney, *English Blue and White
Porcelain of the 18th Century*, London, 1963,
pl 52A.

See colour plate XIV

183 Jug
Liverpool (Richard Chaffers's factory), about
1760–1765
Height 8¾ in (22 cm); diameter of neck 4½ in
(11.5 cm)

Jug with swelling body above a foot broader
than the neck, which has a large beaked spout;
tagged strap handle.
Painted in enamel-colours with five birds
mobbing an owl, watched by a peacock on a
tree on one side, two golden pheasants on the
other.

Illustrated in *ECC Trans*, vol 5, pt 5, 1964,
pl 253A; G. Wills, *English Pottery and
Porcelain*, Guinness Signature Series, London,
1969, colour pl 43.

184 Punch-bowl

Liverpool (Philip Christian's factory), about 1765
Height 4⅜ in (10.7 cm); diameter 10¼ in (26 cm)

Painted in underglaze-blue with a partially wrapped sugar-loaf within a diaper border inside; outside, with a fence and flowering plants in Chinese style. Inscribed: 'Success to the Greenock Shugar House'.

Illustrated in *ECC Trans*, vol 6, pt 2, 1966, pl 58B.

Exhibited at the Fitzwilliam Museum, Cambridge (1967).

The first sugar-factory in Greenock was erected about 1765 at the foot of Sugar House Lane.

185 Flower-pot

Liverpool (Seth Pennington's factory), dated 1780
Height 5⅝ in (14.5 cm)

Flower-pot with out-turned rim and hole in base.
Painted in underglaze-blue with sailing-ships off the coast flying British flags, scrollwork below. Inscribed: 'WD 1780'.

Illustrated in Bernard Watney, *English Blue and White Porcelain of the 18th Century*, London, 1973, pl 61B.

Exhibited at the Fitzwilliam Museum, Cambridge (1967).

Caughley Porcelain

186 Tureen, Cover and Stand
Caughley, about 1775
Height overall 4⅛ in (10.5 cm); length of stand
9¼ in (23.5 cm)

Almost straight-sided tureen of four-lobed plan,
with cover and stand of matching shape, the
cover having a handle formed of conjoined
stems with leaf-terminals.
Painted in underglaze-blue with small Chinese
scenes on square scrolls reserved against sprays
of flowers and leaves. Similar sprays decorate
the rim of the stand and the top of the cover,
while the rim of the cover and the *cavetto* of the
stand are decorated with a diaper border
interrupted by panels enclosing Chinese pearl-
and lozenge-symbols.

For the shape cf. G. Godden, *Caughley and
Worcester Porcelains, 1775–1800*, London, 1969,
fig 207.

187 Pair of Large Jugs
Caughley, about 1775–1780
Height 9¼ in (23.5 cm) and 8¾ in (22.5 cm)

Ovoid jugs with 'cabbage-leaf' moulding, the
cylindrical necks with mask-spouts; loop
handles moulded with scrolls top and bottom.
Printed in underglaze-blue with three large, and
various smaller, sprays of flowers and leaves,
and inscribed in underglaze-blue: 'Robt
JEFFREYS SALOP' and
'Edw.JEFFREYS.SALOP'.

Exhibited at the Loan Exhibition of Shropshire
Antiquities, Shrewsbury, 1898, *Cat*, Section II,
no 30; and in the Bicentenary Exhibition of
Caughley Porcelain *Catalogue*, II, no 30;
Shrewsbury Museums, 1972, no 11.

Edward (1720–1801) and Robert (1717–1800)
Jeffreys were the sons of the Revd. Edward
Jeffreys, Vicar of Ruyton-XI-Towns.
Robert Jeffreys was a former Vicar of
Whitchurch.

188 Jug
Mark: Royal Arms, in relief, impressed.
Hard-paste Caughley or Coalport, about 1799
Height 8 in (20.2 cm); diameter of neck 3½ in
(9 cm)

Jug of inverted baluster form, with cylindrical
neck, mask-lip and triple-scrolled handle, the
body with 'cabbage-leaf' moulding.
Printed in underglaze-blue with a parrot
perched on a branch pecking grapes ('Parrot
and Fruit' design), and a secondary print
showing a bunch of grapes, together with floral
sprays incorporating pine-cones on the neck.

Exhibited at the *Bicentenary Exhibition of
Caughley Porcelains*, Shrewsbury Museums,
1972, no 397.

The fragment stamped with the same Royal
Arms mark and shown with this jug, was found
on the site of the Caughley factory, and
although it is itself of soft-paste porcelain, it
suggests that the jug is probably of Caughley
origin, in which case the date would be
1798–1799: if of Coalport origin (John Rose's
factory), the date would be 1799–1802.

189 Pair of Dessert-dishes
Mark: 'Powell 91 Wimpole Street'
Caughley, about 1790, decorated in London
about 1820
Width 8 in (20.5 cm)

Three-lobed dishes with radiating curved ribs
and shell-moulded handles.
Painted in enamel-colours with peasant-figures,
described underneath the bases as 'Paysanne de
la Forêt Noire' and 'Canton Soleure'. The rims
are decorated with a greenish-blue band
between gilt borders.

For Powell's of Wimpole Street, see W. B.
Honey, *Old English Porcelain*, London, 1948,
p 216.

Lowestoft Porcelain

190 Leaf Dish
Lowestoft, about 1760
Length 6¼ in (16 cm)

Dish in the shape of a large currant-leaf on
which are superimposed three smaller leaves and
sprays of currants in relief, the loop handle
formed by a stalk.
Painted in underglaze-blue with a scroll-border.

The shape is taken from salt-glazed stoneware
(see B. Rackham, *Catalogue* of the Schreiber
Collection, II, London, 1930, no 142).

191 Tea-caddy and Cover
Lowestoft, about 1770
Height 4½ in (11.5 cm)

Baluster shape with collar neck and low domed
cover surmounted by a four-petalled flower
finial.
Painted in pink enamel with two Chinese
figures, one playing a lute and one standing by a
table on which is a flower in a vase, a tree in the
background. Cell-diaper borders round the
shoulder of the caddy and the rim of the cover.

Illustrated in G. A. Godden, *The Illustrated
Guide to Lowestoft Porcelain*, London, 1969,
pl 166; J. Howell, 'Some Notes on the
Introduction of Polychrome Decoration at
Lowestoft'. *ECC Trans*, vol 9, pt 3, 1975,
pl 162C.

192 Coffee-jug and Cover
Lowestoft, about 1755
Height 9¾ in (24.7 cm)

Pear-shaped body with lip-spout and strainer, and scroll handle with thumb-rest. The low domed cover has a bun knob.
Painted in enamel-colours and gilt, with a large spray of flowers in which an orange tulip is prominent, and a smaller spray of flowers on the cover. Gold arcaded border, and touches of gold on the handle, cover-knob, etc.

Illustrated in the *Catalogue* of the exhibition below, pl II; *Saturday Book*, no 18, 1958, p 73; J. Howell, 'Some notes on the Introduction of Polychrome Decoration at Lowestoft', *ECC Trans*, vol 9, pt 3, 1975, pl 165B.

Exhibited at the Lowestoft China Bicentenary Exhibition, Christchurch Mansion, Ipswich, 1957.

Painted by the 'Tulip Painter'.

Formerly in the Noel H.P. Turner Collection.

193 Salt-cellar
Lowestoft, about 1775
Height 1¾ in (4.5 cm); diameter 2¾ in (7 cm)

Round, incurved bowl with three lion-masks
and paw feet.
Painted in underglaze-blue with a floral and leaf
festoon, and a loop border.

Cf. Bernard Watney, *English Blue and White
Porcelain of the 18th Century*, London, 1973,
pl 81C; G. Godden, *The Illustrated Guide to
Lowestoft Porcelain*, London, 1969, pl 92.

194 Teapot and Cover
Lowestoft, about 1775
Height 6 in (15 cm)

Ovoid teapot with plain loop handle, slightly
curved spout, and low domed cover with
flattened spherical knob.

Painted in enamel-colours (red, green and
brown) with goldfish amidst plants, the details
picked out in gold.

195　Coffee-pot
Lowestoft, about 1780
Height 10½ in (26.8 cm)

Pear-shaped body with curved spout and scroll
handle with thumb-rest. Domed cover with
bun-knob.
Painted in blackish sepia enamel ('pencilled')

and gilt, with a Chinese root, fence and peony
design.

Illustrated in M. L. Powell, *Lowestoft China*,
Lowestoft, 1934, front cover.

Said to have been made as part of a wedding
service for Hewlin Luson's son, also Hewlin

Luson, who married Rebecca Kippen at
Lowestoft on 2 March 1777.

From the Hewlin Luson, M. L. Powell and
G. W. Middleton Collections (Sotheby's,
23 October 1973, Lot 64).

196 Vase
Plymouth, 1768–1770
Height 7⅞ in (20 cm)

Tall ovoid vase with low neck.
Painted in dark underglaze-blue with two
vertical oval panels enclosing Chinese
river-scenes; between the panels are flowering
plants.

Exhibited at the Fitzwilliam Museum,
Cambridge (1967).

197 Tankard
Plymouth, about 1770
Height 6¼ in (16 cm)

Bell-shaped tankard with fluted loop-handle and
heavy foot.
Painted in enamel-colours with the figures of a
Chinese man and woman seated on a bench
reading a musical score, and flanked on either
side by two other standing figures.

**198 Pair of Figures of a Boy with a Dog
and a Girl with a Dog**
Bristol (Richard Champion's factory), about
1770–1775
Height of Boy 7⅛ in (18 cm); height of
girl 7½ in (19 cm)

The laughing Boy points with his left hand at a
dog which he holds on a tree-stump to his right,
with his hat placed on the dog's head. The Girl
also holds her dog on a tree-stump to her left,
her hat on its head. Both figures stand on
rockwork bases.
Painted in enamel-colours and gilt, the Boy
wearing a white jacket figured with red
flower-sprays and elaborate gilt borders, green
breeches and blue shoes with red rosettes. The
Girl wears a white skirt with red flower-sprays
and elaborate gilt borders, green jacket, puce
sash and a feathered gold circlet on her hair.

Cf. Arthur Lane, *English Porcelain Figures of the
18th Century*, London, 1961, p 127; F. Severne
MacKenna, *Champion's Bristol Porcelain*,
Leigh-on-Sea, 1947, fig 94; B. Rackham,
Catalogue of the Schreiber Collection, I,
London, 1928, no 748, pl 84.

The model is almost certainly by Pierre
Stephan. The examples in the Schreiber
Collection bear the impressed 'T⁰' mark of the
'repairer' Tebo (see no 199).

199 Figure of a Boy Playing a Hurdy-Gurdy
Mark: 'T⁰', impressed
Bristol (Richard Champion's factory), about
1772–1774
Height 7¾ in (19.7 cm)

The Boy stands with left foot advanced and his
head on one side: he is supported by a tree
stump and stands on a rocky base.
Painted in enamel-colours and gilt, the blue hat
trimmed with an orange feather, blue rosettes
on black shoes and puce cuffs.

See Arthur Lane, *English Porcelain Figures of
the 18th Century*, London, 1961, p 127;
F. Severne MacKenna, *Champion's Bristol
Porcelain*, Leigh-on-Sea, 1947, fig 96.

The model is almost certainly by Pierre
Stephan, the 'T⁰' mark being that of the
'repairer' Tebo.

200 Teapot and Cover
Bristol (Richard Champion's factory), about
1775
Height 6¼ in (15.5 cm)

Teapot of ogee profile with curved spout, low
domed cover with flower finial, and ear-shaped
handle with thumb-piece.
Painted in enamel-colours and gilt with 'harbour
scenes' in puce monochrome below a formal
border in red and gold, repeated on the cover.

See for the decoration W. B. Honey, *Old
English Porcelain*, London, 1948, pl 108C.

201 Flask
Hard-past New Hall, about 1782–1785
Height 4¼ in (11 cm); diameter of body 3¾ in
(9.5 cm)

Circular flattened flask with short cylindrical
neck and flattened base.
Painted in enamel-colours on each face with a
central bouquet of flowers and leaves within a
pink 'pseudo-scale' border.

202 Part Tea Service
Hard-paste New Hall, about 1782–1785
The service consists of:

Teapot, Cover and Stand, height 6½ in
(16.5 cm), globular body with 'clip' handle and
curved spout, and flat cover with pointed finial
picked out in gold.

Tea-caddy and Cover, height 4⅞ in (12.5 cm),
of ovoid form with pointed finial.

Slop Bowl, diameter 6⅛ in (15.5 cm).
Bread and Butter Plates in two sizes, 7⅞ in
(20 cm) and 8½ in (21.5 cm).

Coffee Cups with 'clip' handles, height 2⅝ in
(6.7 cm).

Tea Bowls, diameter 3⅜ in (8.5 cm).
Saucers, diameter 5⅛ in (13 cm).

Painted in sepia and iron-red enamels with
figures in landscapes. Painted by Fidelle
Duvivier.

See G. Grey in (ed) R. J. Charleston, *English
Porcelain*, 1745–1850, London, 1965, pl 61B;
David Holgate, *New Hall and its Imitators*,
London, 1971, pl 16.

From the H. Page Cross Collection.

See colour plate XV

203 Teapot and Cover
Hard–paste New Hall, about 1782–1787
Height 6½ in (16.5 cm); length 8½ in (21.5 cm)

Globular teapot on pedestal foot, with curved
spout and scrolled handle, the spout with leaf
moulding round the base and the upper part of
the handle with four raised husks. The low
domed cover has an acorn finial rising from six
radiating oak-leaves in relief.
Painted in enamel-colours with a Chinese boy
holding a windmill, offering a flower to a lady
standing beneath a parasol by a fence in a
garden; scattered floral sprigs on the cover
(pattern 20).

Illustrated in David Holgate, *New Hall and Its
Imitators*, London, 1971, colour pl C, and
discussed *ibid*, p 35.

Exhibited Northern Ceramic Society Exhibition,
Leeds, 1947, no 92.

204 Cream Boat
Hard-paste New Hall, about 1782–1787
Height 2⅞ in (7.5 cm); length 4¾ in (12 cm)

Oval on plan with tall pouring lip and
overlapping handle with thumb piece, the body
moulded with leaf motifs in relief between
grooves rising spirally from the base ('Low
Chelsea Ewer').

Painted in enamel-colours (pink, blue and
green) with small star-like flower sprigs and
quatrefoil motifs, alternately blue and pink,
used as a border. The relief-moulded leaves are
picked out in green with pink veins.

Illustrated in David Holgate, *New Hall and Its
Imitators*, London, 1971, pl 3.

205 Punch-bowl
Hard-paste New Hall, about 1785
Height 4⅞ in (12.5 cm); diameter 12½ in
(31.8 cm)

Hemispherical bowl on tall collar foot.
Painted in enamel-colours and gilt, with a
border inside of rose sprigs framed in tasselled
gilt pendants (a current factory pattern, no 83)
used to set off a central rose spray.

For the pattern see David Holgate, *New Hall
and Its Imitators*, London, 1971, colour pl D.

206 Jug
Hard-paste New Hall, about 1785–1790
Height 7¾ in (19.7 cm)

Presentation jug, with an ovoid, slightly waisted body and spreading foot, high cylindrical collar with projecting lip leaf-moulded underneath, and characteristic triple-scroll handle.

Painted in enamel-colours with a rose spray on one side and with three bell-like flowers in pink on S-curved stems on the reverse. Gilt husk and scroll motif below the lip, and gilt lines on the rim, foot and handle, with the initials 'AB' intertwined on the front of the body.

207 Jug

Hard-paste New Hall, about 1795–1803
Height 7¾ in (19.5 cm)

Ovoid jug with low spreading foot, collar neck
with pouring spout, and elaborately scrolled
handle. Transfer-printed overglaze in puce with
the Farmer's Arms between a reaper and a
mildmaid as supporters, inscribed 'THE
FARMERS ARMS' and 'IN GOD IS OUR

TRUST'. On the reverse is the inscription:
'SUCCESS TO THE PLOUGH THE FLEECE
AND THE PAIL: MAY THE LANDLORD
EVER FLOURISH AND THE TENANT
NEVER FAIL', within a border of farm
implements. On the front, 'TB' monogram in
gold.

See for the shape David Holgate, *New Hall and
Its Imitators*, London, 1971, pls A–B (handle),

13A, 16.
Exhibited at the Northern Ceramic Society
Exhibition, Leeds, 1974, no 115.

No other example of on-glaze transfer-printed
hard-paste New Hall porcelain appears to be
recorded and the printed decoration may have
been added outside the factory.

Eighteenth Century Porcelain of Uncertain Origin

208 Cream-jug
London, perhaps Chelsea, 'Girl-in-a-Swing'
factory, about 1751–1754
Height 3¼ in (8 cm)

Baluster-shaped cream-jug moulded with curved
diagonal gadrooning, having a crabstock handle,
and a base decorated with applied strawberries
and leaves in relief.
Painted in enamel-colours with two
flower-sprays (tulip and peony) a sprig and two
insects, the relief decoration being picked out in
red, black and two tones of green.

Illustrated in Bernard Watney, 'A Hare, A
Ram, Two Putti and Associated Figures',
ECC Trans, vol 8, pt 2, 1972, p 227, pl 183B.

**209 Group of Ganymede and the Eagle,
made as a Candle Sconce**
London, perhaps Chelsea, 'Girl-in-a-Swing'
factory, about 1751–1754
Height 7½ in (19 cm); length 6¼ in (16 cm)

Ganymede sits with his left arm round the
eagle's neck, both on a rockwork base, with
candle-holder formed of overlapping leaves, and
having applied leaves round the base of it.

See Arthur Lane and R. J. Charleston,
'Girl-in-a-Swing porcelain and Chelsea',
ECC Trans, vol 5, pt 3, 1962, p 139, no 2E.

Exhibited ECC, 1948 (*Exhibition Catalogue*,
no 253).

This group would originally have formed a pair
with a 'Europa and the Bull', (see no 210).

210 Group of Europa and the Bull, made as a Candle Sconce

London, perhaps Chelsea, 'Girl-in-a-Swing' factory, about 1751–1754
Height 7½ in (19 cm); width 6¾ in (17.5 cm)

Europa sits on the back of the bull, who is garlanded with flowers in relief, the candle-holder made of overlapping leaves and having applied leaves around the base of it.

See Arthur Lane and R. J. Charleston, 'Girl-in-a-Swing porcelain and Chelsea', *ECC Trans*, vol 5, pt 3, 1962, p 139, no 3D.

This group would originally have formed a pair with a 'Ganymede and the Eagle' (see no 209).

211 Pair of Figures, a Girl with a Basket and a Boy with a Fish, Emblematic of Earth and Water

London, perhaps Chelsea, 'Girl-in-a-Swing' factory, about 1751–1754

Height of Girl 8½ in (21.5 cm); height of Boy 8 in (20.5 cm)

The Girl stands with her left leg advanced, holding in both hands a basket of flowers. The Boy stands with left leg advanced, his right resting on a tree-stump, and holds a large fish in both hands. Both figures stand on wide circular plinths with slightly undercut bevelled edges.

See Lane and Charleston, *loc. cit.*, above, pp 141–142, items 14 and 15.

212 Saucer and Stand

Marks: 'A' in underglaze-blue on both
Perhaps Vauxhall (Nicholas Crisp's factory), or
Gorgie (Alexander Lind's factory), about
1750–1755
Diameter 4½ in (11.5 cm) and 4⅞ in (12.5 cm)

Painted in enamel-colours (brown, blue, yellow,
purple and iron-red) with two scenes
surrounded by rococo scrollwork in iron-red –
'Hob surprised by Sir Thomas with
Mr. Friendly's Letter' and 'Friendly as a Ballad
Singer at ye Country Wake'.

Illustrated in R. J. Charleston and J. V. G.
Mallet, 'A Problematical Group of 18th Century
Porcelains', *ECC Trans*, vol 8, pt 1, 1971,
pls 78–79, and discussed, *ibid*, pp 80ff.

The subjects are taken from engravings by G.
Bickham, after H. Gravelot, illustrating John
Hippisley's opera *Flora*.

Hard-paste Porcelain of Foreign Origin Decorated in London

213 Jug

Chinese hard-paste porcelain decorated in
London, about 1755–1760
Height 3½ in (8.5 cm)

Pear-shaped jug with plain loop handle and faint
diaper moulding below the rim.
Painted in enamel-colours with two bulls
charging each other, in a landscape with trees.

Perhaps painted by Jefferyes Hamett O'Neale.

214 Teapot, Cover and Stand

Chinese hard-paste porcelain decorated in
London, about 1755–1760
Height of teapot 5⅛ in (13 cm); width of stand
5⅛ in (13 cm)

Globular teapot with plain loop-handle, straight
spout, and low domed cover with pear-shaped
knob. Hexagonal lobed stand.
Painted in enamel-colours with Fable scenes
(the Horse and the Ass on the teapot and the
Fox and the Grapes on the stand), a river
landscape on the cover.

Perhaps painted by Jefferyes Hamett O'Neale,
and clearly inspired by Chelsea porcelain.

215 Tea-bottle
Chinese hard-paste porcelain decorated in
London, about 1755–1760
Height 4 in (10.2 cm); diameter of foot 1⅞ in
(5 cm)

Jar of baluster-shape with low neck and
open-work foot of applied scrolls.
Painted in enamel-colours with sprays of flowers
and leaves, with insects.

Cf. Bernard Watney, 'The King, the Nun, and
other Figures, *ECC Trans*, vol 7, pt 1, 1968,
pls 58C and D, 59A to C.

216 Group Symbolic of Air, from a Set of the Elements
Meissen hard-paste porcelain decorated in
London; about 1750–1754
Height 6¾ in (17 cm); length 6¼ in (16 cm)

The group consists of a woman reclining on a
rockwork base, with flying hair, a bird perched
on her left hand. Behind her are two *putti*, one
flying on a cloud with a bird on his hand and
the other working a pair of bellows.
Painted in enamel-colours, those on the hair and
draperies having been applied at the Meissen
factory, those used for the flower-sprays added
in London.

Cf. Arthur Lane and R. J. Charleston,
'Girl-in-a-Swing porcelain and Chelsea',
ECC Trans, vol 5, pt 3, 1962, pp 116–117,
pls 132B and C, 133A and B; and Bernard
Watney, 'The King, the Nun, and other
Figures', *ibid*, vol 7, pt 1, 1968, pls 60A and B,
61 and 62A and B.

This group appears to have been painted by the
enameller who painted most of the
'Girl-in-a-Swing' porcelain (cf. no 208).
A Meissen figure painted by the same hand is in
the Museum of Fine Arts, Boston (Lane and
Charleston, pl 132B).

217 Plant-pot and Stand
Pinxton, about 1796–1799
Height with stand 6½ in (16.5 cm); diameter of rim 6¼ in (15.7 cm)

Flower-pot shape with attached ring handles and hole in base, standing on a spreading holder to take surplus water.
Painted in enamel-colours with a castle in landscape (identified as 'Haddon Hall Derbys' in gold on the base) within gold borders, reserved on a pink-beige ground painted with classical vases, swags, etc. in sepia. On the reverse, an oval panel painted with flowers in a basket. Over both panels is a Duke's coronet.

218 Pair of Bough Pots
Pinxton, about 1796–1799
Height 5¼ in (13.2 cm); width 7 in (17.5 cm)

Semicircular holders standing on bracket feet, the separate covers with three nozzles for bulbs and four holes for cut flowers.
Painted in natural enamel-colours with landscapes in rectangular panels reserved on a white ground with ornate gilt scrollwork. The landscapes are named as 'Chepstowe Castle, Monmouthshre' and 'Harlech Castle, Merionethshre'.

Illustrated in W. D. John, *William Billingsley*, Newport, 1968, colour pl 7B; see also *The Connoisseur*, February 1963, pp 82, 87.

The painting is attributed to Williams Billingsley.

From the Coke Collection.

219 Beaker

Mark: 'Billingsley Mansfield', painted in puce
enamel.
Porcelain of uncertain origin, perhaps Caughley,
decorated by William Billingsley in Mansfield.
Height 4⅛ in (10.5 cm)

Straight-sided beaker tapering towards the foot.
Painted in enamel-colours with a mountainous
landscape identified by an inscription below the
foot as 'View of Matlock High Tor'. The
reverse bears the monogram 'I.H.' in gold.

Illustrated in W. D. John, *William Billingsley*,
Newport, 1968, pl 52A.

Formerly in the Sydney Heath and W. D. John
Collections.

220 Breakfast Cup and Saucer

Torksey, about 1808
Height of cup 2¼ (5.5 cm); diameter of saucer
6½ in (16.5 cm)

Hemispherical cup with angled handle of square
section.
Painted in enamel-colours (blue, iron-red, pink,
green, yellow with some black outlining) with a
crude 'Japan' pattern, including a central 'sun
burst' and a floral spray.

The attribution is based on a cup and saucer in
the Victoria and Albert Museum (C437, 1920)
with a strong traditional ascription to Torksey.
It is decorated with the same pattern, and has
the same angular handle. Fragments of similar
handles have been excavated on the Torksey site
(Brampton).

221 Sucrier and Cover
Nantgarw, about 1816
Height 4⅝ in (11.5 cm)

Depressed hemispherical body with shoulder of
concave profile, standing on a low foot, and
with plain loop handles. The sloping cover has a
gilt pineapple knob.
Painted in enamel-colours with continuous
sprays of naturalistic flowers and leaves round
the body and cover; gilt husk-border round the
shoulder.

The painting is attributed to Thomas Pardoe.

222 Vase
Nantgarw, about 1816, decorated in London
Height 5 in (12.5 cm)

Low urn-shaped vase with wide shoulder and
narrow neck of concave profile, standing on a
pedestal foot, and with gilt side-handles in the
form of coiled dolphins. The rim of the neck is
gadrooned and the base of the vase and the
upper surface of the foot are decorated with
radiating leaf-mouldings.
Painted in enamel-colours with an elaborate
border of naturalistic flowers and leaves round
the neck. Elaborate gilt borders.

See for the shape, W. D. John, *Nantgarw
Porcelain*, Newport, 1948, pl 16B.

Formerly in the Harry Sherman Collection.

223   Cabinet Cup and Saucer
Mark: 'Swansea', painted in gold
Swansea, about 1814–1815
Height of cup 3⅜ in (8.5 cm); diameter of
saucer 6 in (15 cm)

Cylindrical cup with everted rim and heavy
footrim, the snake-handle with moulded lower
part.
Painted in enamel-colours with floral bouquets,
one on the cup and two on the saucer, in
rectangular panels truncated at the corners and
bordered with gold lines. Gold floral and diaper
borders.

See for the shape, W. D. John, *Swansea
Porcelain*, Newport, 1958, pl 14A.

Exhibited at the Glyn Vivian Art Gallery,
Swansea.

The painting is attributed to William
Billingsley.

224   Plate
Mark: 'SWANSEA' over a trident, impressed
Swansea, about 1815, probably decorated in
London
Diameter 9 in (23 cm)

Painted in enamel-colours with a naturalistically
rendered vase of flowers, with fruits and
mushrooms, within circular gilt borders.

Exhibited at the National Exhibition of Works
of Art, Leeds, 1868, no 2383.

From the Rev. T. Staniforth Collection.

225 Tureen and Cover
Mark: 'Swansea', painted in magenta
Swansea, about 1816
Height 6⅛ in (15.5 cm)

Hemispherical bowl-shaped tureen with pedestal foot, mounted on a circular plinth with three gilt paw feet and classical motifs in relief; three gilt lion masks in relief on the body and gilt pineapple knob on the flat cover.
Painted in enamel-colours round the body with a running scroll of naturalistic flowers and leaves, and similar smaller borders on the cover and foot; classical scroll and leaf borders in gold.

Illustrated in Peter Hughes, 'The French Influence on Swansea and Nantgarw Porcelain', *The Connoisseur*, April 1975. See for the shape, W. D. John, *Swansea Porcelain*, Newport, 1958, pl 12D.

The painting is attributed to David Evans.

226 Vase
Mark: 'SWANSEA' and a trident, impressed
Swansea, about 1817, decorated in London
Height 10½ in (26.5 cm)

Elongated ovoid vase with cylindrical neck
flaring at the rim, standing on a square plinth;
side-handles terminating above in fan-like gilt
palmettes.
Painted in enamel-colours with bouquets of
flowers in baskets on the body, floral wreaths
tied in pink ribbons on the neck. Round the
shoulder, base and foot of the vase are borders
of gilt dotted scrollwork.

See for the shape, W. D. John, *Swansea
Porcelain*, Newport, 1958, pl 43–44.

Bone China

227 Dessert Dish
Mark: 'Spode' in brown
Stoke-on-Trent (Spode factory), about 1810
Width 8¼ in (21 cm)

Square dish with indented corners, the *cavetto*
circular.
Painted in enamel-colours with a view of a
pottery with bottle-kilns, possibly the Spode
works, with a gilt formal border.

Exhibited Church Farm House Exhibition,
Hendon, 1974.

228 Pair of Coffee-cans and Saucers
Mark: simulated Sèvres mark with letter 'M'
and 'No 539', in blue enamel
Stoke-on-Trent (Minton factory), about 1810
Height of cans 2½ in (6.3 cm); diameter of
saucers 5½ in (14 cm)

Cylindrical cans with ring handles.
Painted in enamel-colours (blue, green, yellow,
iron-red, orange, rose-pink, brown) with
chinoiserie figures in landscapes, between trees
or gigantic plants. Gilt borders and handles.

See G. Godden, *Minton Pottery and Porcelain of
the First Period, 1793–1850*, London, 1968,
figs 14 and 34, showing the same pattern on
other shapes.

229 Dessert Plate

Mark: 'WEDGWOOD', printed in red
Etruria (Wedgwood factory), about 1813
Diameter 7½ in (19 cm)

Moulded with pairs of shallow ribs giving
alternating narrower and broader lobes at the rim.
Transfer-printed in black and enamelled in
proper colours with a rendering of *Crocus
Biflorus*, or the yellow-bottomed white crocus.

The botanical decoration is accurately copied
from Henry C. Andrews, *Botanists' Repository*,
VI, 1 April, 1804, pl 362 and is referred to as
'Botanical Flowers with Gold diamond border'
(pattern no 681), in the factory's Second Pattern
Book. The same series of floral prints was first
used by Wedgwood in 1810 for underglaze-blue
printed decoration. See J. K. des Fontaines,
'Underglaze blue-printed Earthenware . . .',
ECC Trans, vol 7, pt 2, 1969, pl 139C.

230 Pair of Bough Pots

Mark: an anchor below 'Davenport' on a label,
impressed
Longport (Davenport factory), about 1810
Height 5¼ in (13.5 cm); width 5½ in (14 cm)

Slightly waisted holders of semicircular
section with curved ring-handles.
Painted in enamel-colours (blue, green, yellow,
brown, iron-red and lilac) with landscapes – one
with two figures by a brook, two cottages and a
house in the background, the other with a

manor-house seen across a meadow. Gilt borders
and handles.

See T. A. Lockett, *Davenport Pottery and
Porcelain*, 1794–1887, Newton Abbot, 1972,
pp 102–104, fig 96.

231 Figure of John Liston as Tristram Sappy
Rockingham, about 1826–1830
Height 7½ in (19 cm)

The actor stands with his right hand in his
trouser pocket and the little finger of his left
hand in his mouth.
Painted in enamel-colours and gilt, the tail-coat
pale blue, the waistcoat flowered. The circular
base is inscribed in gold: 'Tristram Sappy, Let
me see, what was I going to say?'.

See D. G. Rice, *The Illustrated Guide to
Rockingham Pottery and Porcelain*, London,
1971, p 78.

John Liston first played the leading role of
Tristram Sappy in 'Deaf as a Post' at Drury
Lane Theatre on 15th February 1823. The
figure is based on a lithograph by George
Maddely.

232 Figure of John Liston as Billy Lackaday
Marks: a griffin printed in reddish sepia and
'No 8' incised under the base.
Rockingham, about 1826
Height 5¼ in (13.5 cm)

The actor in jacket and frilled shirt, leans
forward with his handkerchief in his right

hand, beside a square pedestal.
Painted in enamel-colours and gilt, the jacket
pink, the base washed over in green and
inscribed 'Billy Lackaday' in gold.

Illustrated in D. G. Rice, *The Illustrated Guide
to Rockingham Pottery and Porcelain*, London,
1971, pl 153. John Liston played the leading
role of Billy Lackaday in the opera 'Sweethearts
and Wives', which was first performed at the
Haymarket theatre on 7th July 1823. The figure
was based on a lithograph published by Ingrey
and Maddely.

Enamels

233 Snuff Box
Birmingham or London, about 1750
Diameter 2½ in (6.5 cm); height 1¼ in (3 cm)

Circular box with waisted sides and gilt metal mount.
Painted in colours with floral sprays round the sides and on the base, and on the cover with a 'harbour scene' enclosed within elaborate rococo scrollwork, a gentleman in the foreground saluting a lady (see nos 234–235).

Illustrated in Eric Benton, 'The London Enamellers', *ECC Trans*, vol 8, no 2, 1972, pl 108A.

Exhibited at the Leamington Spa Art Gallery, *Gilt Metal and Enamel Work*, 1967, no 14.

234 Box (perhaps for gaming-counters)
Birmingham or London, about 1750
Length 2⅝ in (6.5 cm); width 2¼ in (5.7 cm); height 1⅜ in (3.5 cm)

Rectangular box with enamel cover and body of mother-of-pearl held together by pinchbeck fillets.
Painted in colours with a 'harbour scene', a gentleman in the foreground saluting a lady (see nos 233, 235).

Illustrated in Eric Benton, 'The London Enamellers', *ECC Trans*, vol 8, no 2, 1972, pl 108D.

Exhibited at the Leamington Spa Art Gallery, *Gilt Metal and Enamel Work*, 1967, no 16.

235 Watch Back
Birmingham or London, about 1750
Diameter 1⅞ in (4.8 cm); height ½ in (1.1 cm)

Painted in colours with a 'harbour scene' enclosed within a border of rococo scrollwork, a gentleman in the foreground saluting a lady (see Nos 233, 234).

Illustrated in Eric Benton, 'The London Enamellers', *ECC Trans*, vol 8, pt 2, 1972, pl 108B.

Exhibited at the Leamington Spa Art Gallery, *Gilt Metal and Enamel Work*, 1967, no 15.

236 Bonbonnière

Birmingham or London, about 1750
Diameter 2⅜ in (6 cm); height 1⅛ in (3 cm)

Circular bonbonnière made in the form of a
basket, with gilt metal base 'rose-engine
turned', the cover of enamel.
Painted in colours with a camp-scene in the
manner of P. Wouwerman, with a horseman in
the centre.

Illustrated in Eric Benton, 'The London
Enamellers', *ECC Trans*, vol 8, no 2, 1972,
pl 104B.

Exhibited at the Leamington Spa Art Gallery,
Gilt Metal and Enamel Work, 1967, no 47.

237 Snuff Box

Probably Birmingham, middle of 18th century
Length 3⅛ in (8 cm); width 2½ in (6.5 cm);
height 1¼ in (3 cm)

Oval box with waisted sides, in pinchbeck
mount.
Painted in colours with flower sprays round the
sides and on the cover with a version of 'The
Singing Lesson'.

Exhibited at the Leamington Spa Art Gallery,
Gilt Metal and Enamel Work, 1967, no 22.

238 Snuff Box

Probably Birmingham, about 1750
Length 2⅝ in (6.5 cm); width 2 in (5 cm)

Rectangular box with gilt metal mounts.
Painted in colours with floral sprays and insects,
the spray on the cover tied with a ribbon.

239 Snuff Box
Probably Birmingham, about 1750
Length 2⅞ in (7.2 cm); width 2 in (5 cm)

Rectangular box with gilt metal mounts.
Painted with rose-sprays and insects within blue
borders over-patterned with gilding. Single
insects are painted inside the cover and on both
sides of the base.

See for the style of decoration, Bernard Watney
and R. J. Charleston, 'Petitions for Patents . . .'
ECC Trans, vol 6, pt 2, 1966, pls 107, 115.

240 Plaque
Probably Birmingham, about 1750
Length 4⅜ in (11 cm); width 3 in (7.5 cm)

Rectangular plaque, perhaps the cover of a
casket.
Painted in colours with insects naturalistically
rendered, in some instances with shadows.

241 Snuff Box
Probably Birmingham, about 1750–1755
Length 3 in (7.5 cm); width 2 in (5 cm); height
1¼ in (3.2 cm)

Rectangular box with bombé sides, mounted in
pinchbeck.
Printed in black, overpainted in colours. On the
cover is a boy drinking with a girl and round
the sides are Italianate landscapes; on the base,
a fly.

The cover design is adapted from a print after
Watteau – see Bernard Watney and R. J.
Charleston, 'Petitions for Patents . . .', *ECC
Trans*, vol 6, no 2, 1966, pl 73C–D; for the
prints on the sides, see *ibid*, pls 64A–B, 97A.

242 Dressing-table Casket
Probably Birmingham, about 1750–1755
Length 10¼ in (26 cm); width 7¼ in (18.5 cm);
height 3¼ in (8.2 cm)

Casket of tinned iron sheet japanned in black
and decorated with formal designs in gold, the
lid set with a panel of enamel secured by an
ornamental gilt metal fillet.
Painted in colours with a Venetian *capriccio* with
shipping in the foreground.

See Therle and Bernard Hughes, *English
Painted Enamels*, London, 1951, fig 71, a set of
three similar boxes; also Bernard Watney and
R. J. Charleston, 'Petitions for Patents . . .',
ECC Trans, vol 6, pt 2, 1966, pls 109C
and 110.

Exhibited at the Leamington Spa Art Gallery,
Gilt Metal and Enamel Work, 1967, no 29
(illustrated).

243 Four Snuff Boxes
Probably Birmingham, about 1750–1760
Diameter 2¼ in (5.5 cm), and 1⅞ in (3.5 cm)

Circular boxes of various materials, including
'Sheffield plate', gilt copper and pressed horn,
the covers of enamel.
Painted in colours with floral sprays and insects.

For further boxes of this type, see Bernard
Watney and R. J. Charleston, 'Petitions for

Patents . . .', *ECC Trans*, vol 6, pt 2, 1966,
pls 111–114, Leamington Spa Art Gallery, *Gilt
Metal and Enamel Work* Exhibition, 1967, pls
facing pp 7, 11, 22.

244 Patch Box
Probably London, about 1755
Length 1⅞ in (4.8 cm); width 1½ in (4 cm)

Rectangular box with gilt metal mounts, and
mirror inside.
Painted in colours with large and small sprays of
flowers and leaves.

See colour plate XVI

245 Patch Box

Probably London, about 1755
Length 2¼ in (5.5 cm); width 1¾ in (4.5 cm);
height ⅝ in (1.5 cm)

Rectangular box with gilt-metal mount and
mirror inside, the sides concave and the cover
slightly domed with corrugations radiating from
the centre.
Painted in colours with a floral spray
surrounded by smaller sprigs, all on a yellow
ground. Inscribed inside: 'Voyez et Souvenez'.

Illustrated in Eric Benton, 'The London
Enamellers', *ECC Trans*, vol 8, pt 2, 1972,
pl 95C.

Exhibited at the Leamington Spa Art Gallery,
Gilt Metal and Enamel Work, 1967, no 89.

See colour plate XVI

246 Patch Box

Probably London, about 1755
Length 2¼ in (5.5 cm); width 1¾ in (4.2 cm);
height ½ in (1.1 cm)

Rectangular box with gilt metal mount and glass
mirror inside.
Painted in colours with a bouquet of flowers on
a dark-blue ground, within a border of gilt
rococo scrollwork: similar gilt scrolls decorate
the sides, and there is a gilt spray on the base.
Inscribed inside 'POUR LA PLUS BELLE', in
gold.

Illustrated in Eric Benton, 'The London
Enamellers', *ECC Trans*, vol 8, pt 2, 1972,
pl 99A–B.

Exhibited at the Leamington Spa Art Gallery,
Gilt Metal and Enamel Work, 1967, no 87.

See colour plate XVI

247 Scent Flask

Probably London, about 1755–1760
Height 2½ in (6.4 cm)

Flask with rectangular body tapering to a
narrow neck, with gilt metal mount.
Painted in gold with sprays of flowers and leaves
on a blue ground.

Illustrated in Eric Benton, 'The London
Enamellers', *ECC Trans*, vol 8, pt 2, 1972,
pl 99C.

Exhibited at the Leamington Spa Art Gallery,
Gilt Metal and Enamel Work, 1967, no 88.

248 Patch Box
Probably London, about 1755–1760
Length 2⅜ in (6 cm); width 2 in (5 cm);
height ⅝ in (1.6 cm)

Oval box with gilt metal mounts and glass mirror inside.
Painted in colours with four exotic birds amidst leafage, in a panel reserved on a blue ground enriched with gold flower sprays: the base is painted with a bouquet of flowers similarly reserved on a blue ground with gilt scrollwork. Inscribed inside 'Gage Damitíè'.

Illustrated in Eric Benton, 'The London Enamellers', *ECC Trans*, vol 9, pt 2, 1972, pl 95A.

Exhibited at the Leamington Spa Art Gallery, *Gilt Metal and Enamel Work*, 1967, no 90.

249 Patch Box
Probably London, about 1755–1760
Length 2⅜ in (6 cm); width 2 in (5 cm);
height ⅝ in (1.6 cm)

Oval box with gilt metal mounts.
Painted in colours with a bird sitting on a peony spray in an irregular oval panel framed by gilt scrollwork and reserved on a green ground with gilt sprays of flowers and leaves. Inscribed inside: 'Lamour et (sic) le Prix'.

Illustrated in Eric Benton, 'The London Enamellers', *ECC Trans*, vol 8, pt 2, 1972, pl 95B.

Probably by a painter who also enamelled blue glass – see Bernard Watney and R. J. Charleston, 'Petitions for Patents . . .', *ECC Trans*, vol 6, pt 2, pp 74–78, pl 68.

250 Snuff Box
Probably London, about 1751–1755
Length 2⅜ in (6 cm); width 1¾ in (4.5 cm);
height 1¼ in (3 cm)

Rectangular box with corrugated top and sides, mounted in gilt metal.
Painted in blue with cornucopias, flowers and wreaths; on the cover in the centre a phoenix and in opposite corners two crowns and two renderings of the Prince of Wales's feathers.

Exhibited at the Leamington Spa Art Gallery, *Gilt Metal and Enamel Work*, 1967, No 86.

This box probably celebrated the creation of the future George III as Prince of Wales on the death of his father Prince Frederick Louis in 1751.

251 Snuff Box
Battersea, about 1753–1756
Length 2¾ in (7 cm); width 2⅛ in (5.5 cm)

Rectangular box with hinged lid and gilt metal mounts.
Printed in magenta brown with on the cover a man and woman with a gun, in a landscape with a dog ('Partie de Chasse'), the sides and base with a diaper trellis.

See Bernard Watney and R. J. Charleston, 'Petitions for Patents . . .', *ECC Trans*, vol 6, pt 2, 1966, pp 90–97, pl 85D.

The inferior quality of the enamel of the base suggests that it may have been printed elsewhere, e.g. Birmingham. The subject is taken from an engraving after a painting by Watteau.

252 Plaque
Battersea, about 1753–1756
Height 4⅛ in (10.5 cm); width 3¼ in (8.5 cm)

Oval plaque in gilt metal mount.
Printed in crimson with profile portrait of George II.

See B. Rackham, *Catalogue* of the Schreiber Collection, III, London, 1924, nos 27, 28, pl 28.

The print is by S. F. Ravenet after the bust engraved by John Sigismund Tanner for the contemporary coinage. Prints are also known in black and in gold with inscription 'Georgius II Rex'.

253 Crucifix
Battersea, about 1753–1756
Height 2¾ in (7 cm), 1⅝ in (4 cm)

Crucifix mounted in gilt metal.
Printed in reddish brown and black,
overpainted with blue, yellow and greyish
brown, with Christ on the Cross looking
upwards.

Cf. another Battersea crucifix showing Christ
looking downwards, illustrated in Bernard
Watney, *Antiques International*, London, 1966,
p 289, fig 3.

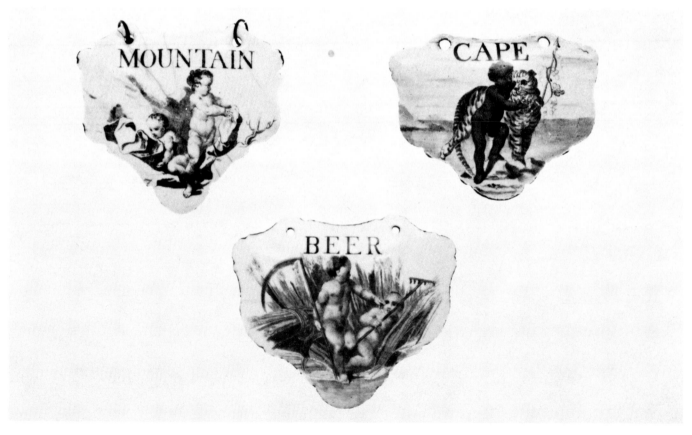

254 Three Wine Labels
Battersea, about 1753–1756
Width 2⅜ in (6.5 cm) to 2⅞ in (7.5 cm)

Escutcheon shape with two holes for suspension.
Printed in brown-red or black, overpainted in
enamel-colours.
1: two *putti* working on a stone quarry,
inscribed 'MOUNTAIN'.
2: a negro boy feeding a leopard with grapes,
inscribed 'CAPE'.

3: two *putti* harvesting barley, inscribed
'BEER'.

The prints are by S. F. Ravenet.

See Cyril Cook, 'The Art and Artists of the
Battersea Enamel Wine-Label', *Connoisseur*,
December 1952, pp 177–180, and March 1959,
p 101, Bernard M. Watney, 'Battersea Wine
Labels; the Present Position', *The Wine Label
Circle Journal*, 5, no 6, December 1973,

pp 133–141; E. W. Whitworth, *Wine Labels*,
London, 1966, p 40.

The design no 2 above is also found on labels
for 'ROTA', no 3 for 'MOUNTAIN', no 1 for
'MALAGA' and 'HONGRIE' (see Rackham,
op cit, pl 40, no 69).

255 Sander from a Desk Set
Perhaps Birmingham, about 1755–1760
Height 1⅞ in (4.5 cm)

Container square on plan, with concave sloping
sides and fluted corners, with gilt metal collar.
Painted in colours with sprays of flowers and
leaves.

256 Five Wine Labels
Probably Birmingham, about 1760
Width (Old Hock) 2⅝ in (6.5 cm)

Labels of various escutcheon shapes.
Painted in colours with flower-sprays and rococo
scrollwork and inscribed 'PERRY', 'HOCK',
'OLD HOCK', 'TONNERRE', 'CHAMPAIN'.

257   Scent Flask
South Staffordshire, about 1760–1765
Height 4 in (10 cm)

Flask of double ogee profile, on a pedestal foot,
and with swelling neck, gilt metal stopper and
finial.
Painted in colours with sprays of flowers within
panels edged with gilt rococo scrollwork and
reserved on a green ground; at the sides a
diaper of white trellis and dot pattern.

See for the shape Therle and Bernard Hughes,
English Painted Enamels, London, 1951,
fig 64C.

Exhibited at the Leamington Spa Art Gallery,
Gilt Metal and Enamel Work, 1967, no 25.

258   Pocket Corkscrew
South Staffordshire, about 1770
Height 4½ in (11.5 cm)

Steel corkscrew with cut-steel loop handle,
screwed into an enamel container.
Painted in colours over raised flower decoration
on a pink ground.

The only recorded example of this form.

259 Snuff Box
Uncertain origin, about 1750
Length 2 in (5 cm); width 1½ in (4 cm)

Rectangular box composed of mother-of-pearl plaques held by fillets of gilt-metal, the top an enamel panel.
Painted in colours with figures of a girl and a boy in a landscape.

260 Badge
Perhaps Liverpool, about 1770–1780
Height 3⅛ in (8 cm); width 2¼ in (5.5 cm)

Oval double-sided badge with gilt metal mount. Printed in black with allegorical scenes within elaborate rococo scrollwork frames – on one side two men carrying a donkey slung on a pole, inscribed 'AVOID RIDICULE'; on the other a man shooting at a stag with a cross bow,

between Fortune and Time as supporters, with a bee-hive as a crest, inscribed 'TRUST IN GOD', 'LEARN BY EXAMPLE', and 'ADHERE TO VIRTUE'.

Perhaps the jewel of an unidentified 18th century Society similar to the Society of Bucks, possibly printed at John Sadler's Liverpool Workshop. Cf. B. Rackham, *Catalogue* of the Schreiber Collection, III, London, 1924,

no 322, pl 41; Bernard Watney, 'Four Groups of Porcelain possibly Liverpool', *ECC Trans*, vol 4, pt 5, 1959, p 22.

261 Plaque
London, dated 1777
Height 6½ in (16.5 cm)

Oval plaque painted in *grisaille* on a purple
ground with a bust of David Garrick placed on
the edge of a rectangular slab decorated with
'Garrick hesitating between Tragedy and
Comedy', amidst trophies of the stage inscribed
'David Garrick left the Stage 1776 after . . .',
and signed 'Wm. Craft 1777'.

William Hopkins Craft (or Croft, c. 1730–1811)
appears to have been an independent enameller,
and executed a number of decorative plaques
and portraits between 1773 and 1802 – see
Aubrey J. Toppin, 'William Hopkins Craft,
Enamel Painter', *ECC Trans*, vol 4, pt 4, 1959,
pp 14–18.
The design 'Garrick between Tragedy and
Comedy' is taken from a painting by Sir Joshua
Reynolds.

Sold at Christie's, 18th May 1965, Lot 46 and
19th December, 1967, Lot 28.